Robert Sommer, Ph.D., is a professor of psychology and director of the Center for Consumer Research at the University of California, Davis. He is the author of numerous books and articles, including *Personal Space* and *Tight Spaces* (Prentice-Hall, Inc.). Dr. Sommer has worked as a consultant on various design projects with private architectural firms as well as with state and federal agencies.

SOCIAL DESIGN

CREATING BUILDINGS WITH PEOPLE IN MIND

Robert Sommer

A SPECTRUM BOOK

Prentice-Hall, Inc.
Englewood Cliffs, N.J. 07632

Library of Congress Cataloging in Publication Data

Sommer, Robert.
Social design.

"A Spectrum Book."
Includes index.
1. Architecture—Human factors—Case studies.
2. Architecture and society—Case studies. I. Title.
NA2542.4.S65 1983 720'.1'03 83-11234
ISBN 0-13-815969-6
ISBN 0-13-815951-3 (pbk.)

A Spectrum Book. Printed in the United States of America.

1 2 3 4 5 6 7 8 9 10

ISBN 0-13-815969-6

ISBN 0-13-815951-3 {PBK.}

Editorial/production supervision: Marlys Lehmann
Cover design: Neil Stuart
Manufacturing buyer: Doreen Cavallo

Prentice-Hall International, Inc., *London*
Prentice-Hall of Australia Pty. Limited, *Sydney*
Prentice-Hall Canada Inc., *Toronto*
Prentice-Hall of India Private Limited, *New Delhi*
Prentice-Hall of Japan, Inc., *Tokyo*
Prentice-Hall of Southeast Asia Pte. Ltd., *Singapore*
Whitehall Books Limited, *Wellington, New Zealand*
Editora Prentice-Hall do Brasil Ltda., *Rio de Janeiro*

To Clara H. Levy,
who asked the grandmother question

CONTENTS

PREFACE

Architecture is a fascinating and difficult subject about which to write. This is why most architects rely on drawings and photographs to describe their work. Yet pictures do not show how a building fits the moods and activities of the occupants. This is a task requiring words. This book is the story of how two groups of people, behavioral scientists and designers, very different in thinking style, temperament, and interests, came together to improve the fit between people and buildings. They shared a belief that knowledge of human behavior would improve the design process and that knowledge about the physical environment would improve the understanding of human behavior. Their association became a microcosm of attempts to apply behavioral science concepts and methods to solve real-world problems.

At various points in the history of architecture, there has been a tendency to judge buildings in terms of physical form by itself. The social design movement introduced occupant satisfaction as another essential criterion of design success. Today there is a tendency to use productivity measures as the "bottom line" of success. This is not an unhealthy development, but there is a danger that quality-of-life yardsticks may be lost in the process. There are many aspects of design that cannot properly be converted into dollar terms, at least according to accepted standards of scientific proof. However, there still is a role for design researchers in demonstrating linkages between design elements and proximate aspects of building use and satisfaction.

My association with architects goes back twenty-five years. I hope that the lessons learned will be of benefit to practical designers and students, colleagues in the behavioral sciences, and to all those who care about the form and functions of buildings. I have deliberately avoided *ad hominem* arguments because I don't feel that they are effective in changing attitudes, except in a negative direction. There is no better way to improve the quality of buildings and neighborhoods than to create a vital constituency for good design among the public.

I have borrowed ideas and methods from too many people to list them all in a preface, so I will leave the evidence of my indebtedness to the text. I am particularly appreciative of the students and faculty in the many schools of architecture, planning, and design where I have lectured. I have also learned important lessons of style, method, and responsibility from the practicing designers with whom I have worked.

Several individuals read this manuscript or portions of it and made helpful suggestions. Foremost among these is my co-conspirator, Barbara Sommer. Thanks are also due to Gwen Baker, Frank Becker, Carla Fjeld, and Mark Francis. Carol Van Alstine did the typing of the various drafts.

Portions of Chapter 11 appeared in the *AIA Journal* and are used with permission.

THE ROAD AWAY FROM FORMALISM

Architecture in 1960 was in a state of technological euphoria. There were new materials, new styles, and abundant work. The nation was in the midst of a major construction boom, and design offices were working around the clock to meet the demand. On campuses, architecture departments were moving from the oldest building to the newest and ugliest. The atmosphere was characterized by buoyancy and optimism. "Architecture is 'in,'" proclaimed Wolf Von Eckardt. "Discussion of new buildings has graduated from newspaper real estate sections to the front page and to all kinds of magazines. Names like Mies Van Der Rohe, Paul Rudolph, Louis Kahn, Philip Johnson, and Ed Stone are dropped at cocktail parties as easily as those of night club performers and golf champions. The American Institute of Architects boasted to its members not long ago that architects have attained such status now that they are featured in whisky ads."[1]

Beneath the surface there was unease and guilt. The architectural heritage of the past century was fast crumbling under the wrecker's ball and chain. Developers, builders, and engineers were taking over many of the roles previously reserved for architects. The planning process was becoming extraordinarily complex and the gulf between designers and occupants was widening. Cities were becoming less humane and habitable as their buildings were designed without amenity, integrity, or delight. People did not like the high-rise buildings that swayed in the wind and created traffic problems and social devastation in the streets. Human scale and neighborhoods were neglected in the quest to reach the stars. Projects receiving the most recognition in awards and feature articles in glossy magazines were corporate skyscrapers of a universal style, vacation homes and condominia for the affluent, and elegant suburban shopping centers. People living in tract houses or small apartments who presumably were most in need of design services had the least access to them. Large segments of the population were finding the work of architects to be irrelevant or hostile to their lives. Traditional methods of city planning were being challenged by communities demanding to participate in decisions that would materially affect them. A growing environmental movement was calling for a re-examination of land-use planning.

New procedures for consultation were needed to cope with

the increased size and complexity of projects. For the Air Force Academy in Colorado, 1700 different items of furniture and equipment had to be selected or designed.[2] The innocent hope that it might be sufficient for a designer to select interiors on the basis of an organizational chart or a list of job descriptions proved shortsighted and mutually frustrating for both designer and occupants. Nor was it sufficient for a city planner to come into a neighborhood scheduled for rehabilitation, ask people what they wanted, and then leave to draw up a plan to be delivered to the city council the following week. Local residents spoke in unfamiliar dialects and made conflicting statements. Some of their desires were unrealistic within existing budgets and political realities. Even white-collar workers were seldom able to explain their space needs in a coherent and consistent manner. Few of them had ever been asked to comment on their buildings. There was not a vocabulary of space shared between occupants and designers. People could not penetrate the architect's jargon, read blueprints or bubble diagrams, or understand furniture catalogs. New techniques had to be evolved to increase the design consciousness of consumers so that they could participate in the planning process. The rapid introduction of new materials and construction techniques, which freed designers from many constraints, raised new questions. Proposals for different types of buildings and interiors could not be answered on the basis of previous experience.

TABLE 1

Progressive Architecture, 1960–1961

Reports in *Progressive Architecture,* which in 1960 boasted of having "the world's largest architectural circulation," convey the elation and expansionism of the period. Everything is new, fresh, booming, up and up, out and away.

January 1960
Saarinen Designs Two New Colleges for Yale . . . Buildings Ready for Winter Olympics . . . Cultural Center Design Shown . . . Americans Design Hospitals for West Berlin . . . Curvaceous Cafe-Club Vaults California Canyon . . . Buildings in Paris Beginning to Reach for Sky.

June 1960
Kahn's Medical Science Building Opens . . . New Las Vegas Air Terminal by Becket . . . Turano's Ideas for Jetports . . . New Theater for Washington . . . Rome Cultural Center Winner.

Continued

TABLE 1 (Continued)
Progressive Architecture, 1960–1961

July 1960 "Delight" from Yamasaki at Seattle 21 . . . Jean Tschumi Wins WHO Headquarters Competition . . . MIT Expansion Plans Announced . . . Proposed "Freedom Monument" Raises Furor . . . Designs for Princeton School of Architecture Shown.
August 1960 Large-Scale Redevelopment in Paris . . . Happy Restoration of Gold Rush Town . . . Tallest Lift-Slab Yet . . . Proposal for Civic Center in Manhattan . . . New Art and Architectural School for Yale by Rudolph.
1961 The P/A Design Awards Banquet Helps Open New University of Minnesota School of Architecture . . . Lozenge-Shaped Insurance Building for Hartford . . . Curtis and Davis Design a Resort Community for Puerto Rico . . . American Architects Create Hotel in Pakistan . . . Spire, Courts, and School for Melbourne Cultural Center . . . "Astronarium and Science Center" Proposed for New York World's Fair . . . Unified Temple for Massachusetts . . . Hawaii: A New Capitol for the Island State . . . Nervi Roofs a Field House at Dartmouth . . . Le Corbusier in the USA . . . *Ad astra per* Concrete with Paul Rudolph Design . . . Gruen's Blockbuster and Columbia's Terraces for Welfare Island . . . Chase Manhattan: The New Cliff in the Lower Manhattan Range.

Among younger architects, there was a growing rejection of formalism, or the tendency to treat buildings as pure shape, without regard to their practical or social functions.[3] Formalists conceived of buildings more as sculpture than as habitat. Architect Philip Thiel characterized his profession as a "charade in which students designed for their professors and practitioners designed for each other, communicating by means of striking photographs in architectural fashion magazines."[4] The formalist position was succinctly stated by Philip Johnson, one of the most influential of today's architects, in his comment, "The job of the architect is to create beautiful buildings. That's all."[5] Johnson echoed the fine arts view of buildings as great hollow sculptures that justified awards based on judgments of architectural photographs that omitted all traces of human presence. The omission of people from photographs of buildings has important consequences for spatial perception. Rudolf Arnheim points out that people can enrich and complete an architectural structure, as water serves a fountain, by conforming to the structure and becoming part of it.[6] Most real buildings look forlorn and incomplete if they are visited after hours when all the occupants have gone. The fact that this is the favored manner of depiction by architectural photographers illustrates the confusion between architecture and sculpture that typifies formalistic design.[7]

Others have likened formalist architecture to painting, especially abstract art. Nicholson and Schreiner describe how English artists in the 1920s and 1930s were influenced by painters of the De Stijl movement, such as Mondrian, who constructed paintings and other constructions out of rectangular areas of primary colors and white and black and lines.[8] Mondrian assembled prototypes of his paintings in movable black strips, and gradually assembled his compositions until they had visual perfection. This approach strongly influenced the architecture of the post-war period.[9] The aesthetic aspect of construction became exclusively a problem of proportions of building cubes and of elements of the outer walls, such as floor heights, articulation of windows, and intervals between supports. Architects assembled two-dimensional plans of houses and models of buildings by the same collage techniques used by Mondrian. It was considered unethical for the viewer of a work of art—or the occupant of a building—to alter in any way the final positioning of the components or to make decisions regarding the outcome.

HELP FROM THE BEHAVIORAL SCIENCES

Architects looked about for assistance in meeting the new concerns about people and buildings. Since most of the issues involved human needs as distinct from problems of form or materials, some architects turned to the social sciences as a means of obtaining reliable information about behavior and well-being. Architecture professors sought from psychologists better answers to questions about the way people experienced buildings. Essential information about the effects of light and color and space were lacking. Richard Neutra, in his book *Survival Through Design,* acknowledged the potential of the behavioral sciences to architecture:

> *With knowledge of the soil and subsoil of human nature and its potentials, we shall raise our heads over the turmoil of daily production and command a view over an earth we shall have to keep green with life if we mean to survive. . . . Tangible observation rather than abstract speculation will have to be the proper guide.*[10]

To document the activities and desires of occupants called for procedures more systematic and rigorous than eyeball inspections or perfunctory discussions with one or two residents. Useful methods were already available to the behavioral scientists, whose basic bag of tricks included interview methods, questionnaires, standardized rating scales, and statistical analysis.

SOCIAL DESIGN

The liaison between design and the behavioral sciences, which we will call *social design,* was part of a larger movement to humanize the process by which buildings, neighborhoods, and cities were planned. Its roots could be traced to Lewis Mumford, Richard Neutra, Jane Jacobs, and Paul and Percival Goodman in architecture and urban planning and Roger Barker, James J. Gibson, and Kurt Lewin in psychology. The movement was not associated with a particular style or aesthetic. The emphasis was more on the process (that is, identifying user values and bringing them into the planning process) than on a specific form or architectural product. The approach was guided by recognition of the designers' responsibility to the people affected by their work. Obviously the client, as the person who signed the contract and paid the bills, was crucial from the standpoint of economic survival. Without clients, an architect will quickly become a nonarchitect. However, the satisfaction of the occupants is critical also for the moral justification of the profession.

What Is Social Design?

On those occasions when I have tried to define social design, I understood the misgivings that a wise old professor of mine had about definitions. Instead of describing things in a sentence or two, he preferred to characterize them. Amos Rapoport said much the same thing: "I am not so much worried any more about 'defining': rather I am interested in 'describing' characteristics . . . according to a number of variables so that the definition of something is not an exact correspondence but a statistical resemblance. When something meets a certain percentage of defining characteristics, then it is considered a representative of the class. When it has lower than this percentage, then it is something else."[11] I believe that social design can be approached in this same way. Rather than offering a tight definition, I will offer the following attributes that set social design apart from conventional design practices.

Social design is working with people rather than for them; involving people in the planning and management of the spaces around them; educating them to use the environment wisely and creatively to achieve a harmonious balance between the social, physical, and natural environment; to develop an awareness of beauty, a sense of responsibility, to the earth's environment and to other living creatures; to generate, compile, and make available information about the effects of human activities on the biotic and physical environment, including the effects of the built environment upon human beings. Social designers cannot achieve these objectives working by themselves. The goals can be realized only within the structures of larger organizations, which include the people for whom a given project is planned.

Landscape designer Mark Francis, whose major professional concern is participatory design of neighborhood parks, has listed the key differences between social design and formalistic design. Some items in Table 2, such as the possibility of lower cost for social design projects, need to be verified through further experience and research. At present there is little factual information available about the relative costs of social design and formalistic approaches. Although user input may be expected to reduce potential misfits between people and buildings, the time and effort required to obtain information about occupants and their activities is not without its costs. Research occupies an important position in the overall agenda of social design.

TABLE 2

Some Key Differences Between Social and Formalistic Design Practice (adapted from Francis[12])

Social Design:	*Formalistic Design:*
• Small Scale	• Large Scale
• Local	• National/International
• Appropriate Technology	• High Technology
• Human-Oriented	• Corporate or Institution-Oriented
• Client Redefined to Include Users	• Owner as Exclusive Client
• Concerned with Meaning and Context	• Concerned with Style and Ornament
• Low Cost	• High Cost
• Bottoms Up Design Approach	• Top Down Design Approach
• Inclusive	• Exclusive
• Democratic	• Authoritarian

Historical Context

Social design was part of a worldwide concern with human rights, based on the assumption that noxious conditions such as poverty, malnutrition, disease, and substandard housing were not inevitable and could be eradicated if sufficient attention and resources were devoted to solutions. This recognition that the good life was possible for all humankind, and not just a privileged few, was not a new philosophical doctrine, since it could be traced back to the utopian thinkers of past ages, but in the 1960s it became a practicable reality for many segments of society previously excluded from the halls of power. In developing nations the struggle centered on colonialism and economic justice, and in the more affluent developed nations, the issues were minority rights and general issues of environmental quality and consumer rights, both broadly defined.

Social design was a means by which those concerned with the built environment could take part in or respond to the human rights movement *as professionals.* Environmental activism had been sparked by books such as Rachel Carson's *Silent Spring,*[13] speeches of Barry Commoner, Paul Ehrlich, and Buckminster Fuller, and the image of the Earth in photographs taken from outer space, confirming that our planet was indeed round, finite, and very small in relation to the solar system. The goals were antipollution laws, protection of endangered species, checks upon unlimited human population growth, conservation of resources, zoning regulations, and other policies directed at quality-of-life issues. Whereas earlier conservation organizations had been concerned largely with protecting the natural environment, particularly forests, lakes, streams, wilderness areas and their natural inhabitants, the interests of the environmental movement included urban and suburban areas. Another concern was reducing demand for scarce, nonrenewable resources through education and legislation. Raised public awareness was seen as a precursor to legislation and a means of reducing unnecessary demands on limited resources. Michael McCloskey, executive director of the Sierra Club, wrote in an editorial in the *Sierra Club Bulletin:*

> *The environmental movement is coming to be more than a relabeled conservation movement. It is coming to represent an amalgamation of many other movements with the conservation movement; the consumer movement, including the corporate reformers; the movement for scientific responsibility, a revitalized public health movement; birth control and population stabilization groups; pacifists and those who stress participatory democracy in which decisions are made consensually; young people who emphasize direct action, and a diffuse movement in search of new focus for politics.*[14]

Other organizations interpreted their objectives in equally broad terms. The consumer movement has been described as an organized expression for an improved quality of life, and to the list of consumer rights was added "the right to a physical environment that will enhance the quality of life."[15] The civil rights movement was part of a worldwide struggle to improve the conditions of the poor. In many parts of the world, this produced revolutions and the emergence of new nations in former colonial territories. Within the United States, it mainly took the form of government programs aimed at improving people's living conditions. Although it was originally termed a civil rights movement because of the struggles of blacks in the southern United States, the goal quickly became extended to economic justice for all segments of the society. Riots in Newark, Detroit, Los Angeles, and other cities brought home to politicians and others that something had to be done to improve the lives of the American underclass. Pragmatically, most tried to do as little as possible in order to quiet the protests and maintain the public order, while still recognizing that some reallocation of goods and services was necessary.

Most of the media attention to the human rights movement of the 1960s was directed to street protests and legislative lobbying. Less attention was paid to changes taking place in the professions in response to the swirling intellectual and ideological currents of the period. Those who sought reform of the professions were imbued with a deep sense of moral purpose. They questioned whose interests were being served and the answer in most cases turned out to be the same. Because of the tendency of social organizations to turn inwards over time and appeal to the segments of society who control the resources, the professions had become self-serving guilds, dependent upon the rich and powerful. Those who were most in need of services had the least access to them. As Frances Moore Lappé pointed out, the marketplace does not respond to need; it just responds to money.[16] This paralleled LeCorbusier's earlier comment that the twentieth century did not build for people; it built for money.[17] There were many unfortunate things that happened in the 1960s, but the increased sense of responsibility among professionals to underserved populations cannot be included among them.

Social design was in part an attempt to reallocate design services to improve the housing and neighborhood needs of the poor. Designers required assistance in meeting the needs of new constituencies with different outlooks, goals, and ways of expressing their wants. The behavioral sciences contributed the concepts, some information, and a social technology for reaching out to underserved populations in what was to be an exciting and perilous journey from the studio into the streets and depressed rural areas. The first issues on which designers and social scientists worked together were the renovation of inner-city neighborhoods, and provision of public housing, migrant worker housing, mental hospitals, geriatric facilities, and institutions for the handicapped. The discontinuity between the old and the new roles for designers was aptly described by F. J. Langdon:

> *When one contrasts the training and client relationships of an 18th century architect and the patron—the grand tour through Italy, the sketch books of Palladian villas and Roman ruins . . . the eventual designing of buildings by a process of discussion and table talk; compared with the brief from a local housing authority for 5,000 low-income tenants or the brief from a speculative developer for a block of multiple tenancy offices—one can only echo the companion of Queen Victoria who remarked after viewing Shakespeare's Antony and Cleopatra, "How very, very different from the home life of our own dear Queen!"*[18]

The social design movement arose to correct misfits between people and the built environment. It was necessitated both by changes in the larger society and in the processes by which buildings, neighborhoods, and cities were planned. The tools and techniques include analysis of user needs prior to starting projects, evaluation of completed buildings, consultation with behavioral scientists, and direct participation by prospective occupants. Before discussing the specific methods, it is necessary to examine the theoretical underpinnings of this approach. There are certain epistemological issues (how we know what we know) that must be dealt with before the value of specific techniques can be considered. It is important to know what the designers wanted to learn from the occupants before assaying the value of the information. Some of the expectations about the potential of behavioral information for improving buildings were unrealistic. Questions of value cannot be answered by any science; science provides information, not advice, and what social scientists could measure was not necessarily interesting or important to architects. Conversely, what architects wanted to know often could not be measured by social scientists, either because a relationship did not exist or because the price tag of the investigation was too high.

Social design did not intentionally ignore the issue of form, except insofar as this was judged by external criteria that had little to do with the lives of the occupants. Imagine a food critic whose main concern is the appearance of the containers in which the food arrives. There are important aspects of the container's shape, size, and color that are properly the concern of marketers who believe, with some justification, that the customer buys the box. Yet the moral justification of the food industry, as indeed of the whole economy, is service to the consumer, and this means primary emphasis must be given to what is inside the package. Form is and should be an important concern among designers, who must judge complexity, levels of meaning, transitions, and coherence. The concerns of the great architects with scale, proportion, and line are equally valid today. Good design requires knowledge about and proper use of materials, site, and structure. For me to emphasize the connection between buildings and their occupants does not imply that these other considerations are unimportant. As a psychologist, I am only doing my job in pointing out that satisfaction of occupant needs is the primary justification of architecture. Loyalty to materials, exciting form, and appropriateness to the landscape are ways of accomplishing this objective. This is an invitation to a greater rather than a lesser vision of architecture.

There is a world of difference between a sculptural chair and one designed to be sat in. Sculptural accessories need only be functional in the most abstract sense of a similarity to the object being depicted. The visitor to the museum exhibition of crafted teacups quickly realizes that no one would use them as teacups, especially since they cost $150 each. They are designed as art objects to be seen and admired. This type of work occupies an honored place in the fine arts. Many eminent painters have attempted to handcraft furniture or accessories whose primary quality is looks. This is a good model for the fine arts but an unsatisfactory one for an applied art such as architecture. "Architecture is not art, at least as we use the word today," declared Canadian architect Moshe Safdie. "Architecture is building environments well."[19] Richard Neutra considered the design of structures to be labor for and *with* occupants. "Human beings must be served and they are reached by design not only as ultimate consumers," Neutra wrote, "they must be won over as co-performers and working crew so that the final design is appealing, both rationally and emotionally."[20]

The inescapable nature of architecture was another justification for social design. People could not vote with their feet to avoid a badly designed city hall or corporate headquarters. Office workers, even management, would have to make do with assigned spaces that interfered with their jobs. In a totally free market, consumers can decide what to accept or reject, but this did not apply in most buildings, rooms, and civic spaces. The relative powerlessness of occupants, their lack of organization, and their inability to express their opinions, created the need for new consulting procedures. Adding to the difficulty was the problem of measuring the effects of building form and layout on performance. If a badly designed building had immediately produced a dramatic deterioration in human health or productivity, the sophisticated survey techniques of the behavioral sciences would have been unnecessary. There was also the need for people in a democratic society to participate in decisions that affected them. It made no sense for people to have input into the political process through their elected representatives and yet lack the ability to influence planning decisions in their own neighborhoods.

How the architectural profession had changed in the course of two decades can be seen in a listing of recent articles from *Progressive Architecture.* Table 3 shows that for 1979 to 1980 the emphasis was on preservation, restoration, energy efficiency, and building small rather than tall. American firms were no longer designing cultural centers in Venezuela and India. They turned inward, emphasizing quality rather than size and fitting in rather than standing out. *Progressive Architecture* no longer proclaimed itself as having "the world's largest architectural circulation."

User participation is not likely to produce radical design solutions. The lengthy discussions and need for compromise are likely to result in only modest incremental departures from conventional wisdom. The master designer or the pop artist hungering for endless novelty is more likely to come up with distinctive forms. Participatory design is not as effective as these other approaches for planning monuments or eye-catching buildings. The goal of social design is to produce buildings and neighborhoods that suit the occupants. Suitability includes aesthetic needs as well as functionality and energy efficiency. The culture of the people tends by its very nature to be conservative, being grounded in available materials and what has gone before.

Social designers are distinguished from their more traditional counterparts by an explicit and primary commitment to the occupants. Their colleagues acknowledge this responsibility in the abstract but in practice operate as if their sole responsibility is to the client who pays the bills. This difference in perceived loyalty is a matter of degree and is not absolute. The litmus test of a social designer is the attempt to obtain *systematic* input from present or future occupants. If there is no attempt to do this, then the project is not social design, no matter how strong are the humanitarian impulses of the architect or the rhetoric contained in the prospectus. The practice of including users directly in the planning process is sometimes described as *participatory design.* However, the movement that arose in the 1960s had a second aspect in addition to user participation, and that was a reliance on behavioral science methods

TABLE 3

Progressive Architecture, 1979–1980
October 1979 Low rise lives: Low rise housing, which is still being built, often offers inventive solutions . . . From the ideal to the real when Marcus Garvey Park Village in Brooklyn, New York is reviewed by PA six years later . . . A new old language. Daniel Solomon and Associates has designed Pacific Heights townhouses in the San Francisco vernacular with the aim of resolving conflicts between new development requirements and preservation ideals . . . Tidewater traditions . . . Traditional weave: Housing in Iran's Shustar new town . . . provides an urban environment that has traditional patterns of social interaction . . . Regional/urban design assistance teams offer design assistance to cities, towns, and rural areas.
April 1980 Energy-conscious design . . . Big problem, small world: Like the U.S., other countries face energy shortages . . . Washington's commitment . . . Architectural energy analysis . . . Rainbow's end . . . Going solar in the city . . . More than just energy . . . Importance of team effort by the architect and the engineer in planning an energy conserving building.
July 1980 The delight deficit . . . The small building artistically considered . . . An addition to the Quail Valley sewage treatment plant in Missouri City, Tx., offers a turn-of-the-century face to neighbors . . . The Flat Rock Brook Center for Environmental Studies in Englewood, N.J., has a central hall that becomes part of a nature path . . . The addition to St. Alban's School relates to both the style and the siting of older buildings on campus . . . The Olean (N.Y.) Fire Station deals with the problem of fitting required spaces to the restricted area . . . uses a building form reflecting its neighborhood . . .

and concepts. The term *social design* reflects the combination of participatory planning methods and social science concepts. A goal of this book is to renew interest in this approach at a time when "bottom-line" concerns (that is, money) are paramount and humane values seem especially vulnerable.

2 MUTUAL CONCERNS OF DESIGNERS AND BEHAVIORAL SCIENTISTS

One of the first tasks in social design was the development of a vocabulary of people in occupied spaces. The fine arts' view of the occupants as spectators at a sculpture exhibit was inappropriate. The term *consumer* was inadequate because of its etymological root meaning to use up or take up wholly, as in eating or destruction, for example, to consume by fire. Most buildings were not consumed by their occupants, at least on a short-term basis. The term *client* refers to those who contract for a project and pay the fees. A century ago they would have occupied the space, but not necessarily today, when they are more likely to be an anonymous hospital board, city agency, or corporate group designing a facility for others. The terms *occupants, users,* and *residents* more aptly describe those who inhabit and are affected by designed spaces. In the ensuing chapters, *designer* will be used in the generic sense of all those professionals such as urban planners, architects, landscape architects, and interior designers whose primary concern is the planning and design of the physical environment. The scale of the designed environment may vary from individual rooms and furnishings to buildings, neighborhoods, and cities. *Behavioral science* refers to those academic fields such as anthropology, psychology, sociology, psychiatry, and human geography that study human attitudes and activities.

It is interesting to approach the liaison between architecture and psychology from the standpoint of personality types. Designers tend to be highly visual people, concerned with practical problem-solving and aesthetics. Psychologists, on the other hand, tend to be highly verbal and abstract, involved more with words than things, and interested in theory and experimentation. The overlap in interest between the two professions was minimal at the outset. Perhaps it was this difference in approach that lay behind their liaison. Neither group was competing with the other for resources or status, as architecture was with engineering or clinical psychology was with psychiatry. For the most part, it was a nonexploitive relationship, but there were risks in the association on each side. For designers to bring in another group of experts could have undermined each group's autonomy and the special claims to expertise professions work so hard to protect, and for social scientists, their scientific standing could have been jeopardized if they had become involved in quick low-budget studies. Fortunately, each side needed something from the other. Designers wanted knowledge of human behavior and social scientists wanted access to the built environment to enhance their theories and research. A few courageous souls were eager to develop a new profession midway between the two fields.

Figure 1 shows the various themes of social design. The two main lines are user input and social scientist input. These are not necessarily related and can occasionally be antagonistic. User input is the direct involvement of occupants in design decisions; social science input is based on expert judgment. Most of what has happened during the past two decades represents some compromise between the two. Social scientists often contributed to the planning process, not so much as white-coated experts making pronouncements on behavior, but as facilitators who attempted to ensure that designers listened to residents and vice versa. They provided architects and planners with techniques for increasing the involvement of potential occupants.

The inclusion of social scientists on the design team rests on several assumptions. Most important is that the experts have useful and relevant knowledge to contribute in a form that is meaningful and timely for designers. Second, there are many projects on which the users themselves may not be available. Third, there is a difference between wants and needs that the users themselves may not recognize or express in a form intelligible to designers. Finally, one or two user representatives may not fairly or adequately represent

FIGURE 1 Divisions of social design.

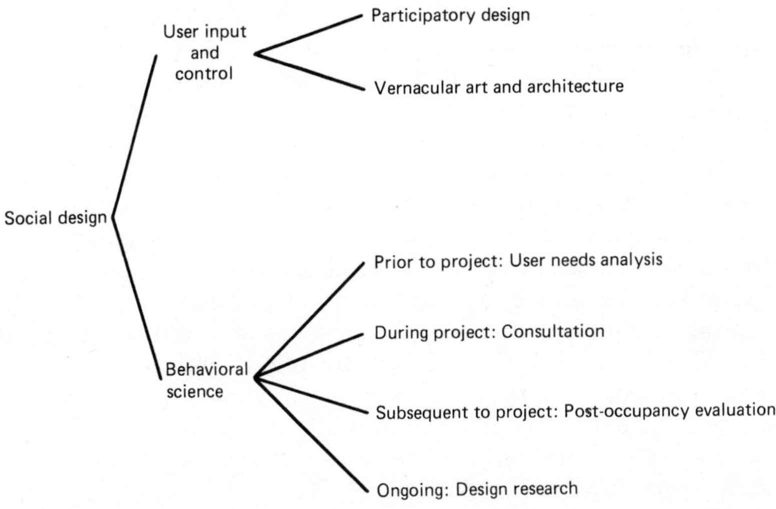

all those who will be affected by a project. Social scientists took part in design sessions not as user surrogates but as consumer advocates.

User input acknowledged the importance of vernacular architecture and art in terms of "learning from the users." Buildings designed and constructed by local residents are more common in developing nations. Anthropologist Amos Rapoport has been concerned with the kinds of shelters built by ordinary people for their daily activities. He defined his purpose as not to romanticize these buildings, but to study them through the concepts and models of the social sciences and to derive lessons that could be applied to contemporary design practice.[1] David Stea found in the squatter settlements in Mexico and Brazil new building forms constructed of materials discarded by nearby city dwellers.[2] These illegal occupations of public or private land by people who had no other alternative shed light on what people feel is essential for shelter and on the creative improvisation of tools, techniques, and materials.

User control over the environment is a somewhat different issue from user design. Control may come about through an exercise in professional judgment or the fact that occupants insist upon it. Opportunities for personalization among housing tenants can be deliberately created, and space outside the buildings can be set aside for community gardens, along with the provision of water sources. Window ledges or other areas receiving natural light can be placed in office buildings to enable workers to care for plants. In institutional buildings, proximate lighting and temperature controls should be installed instead of area-wide systems, along with operable windows and curtains to increase local control over the environment. This is more likely to happen when the residents have some role in the planning process, although it is feasible in top-down design also. However, the client or designer who is sufficiently concerned with occupant control to create "loose fitting spaces" is probably going to make some deliberate effort to involve potential occupants in the planning process as well.

There were six major areas of concern in the early liaison between the design professions and the social sciences: (1) the human use of space; (2) environmental awareness and cognition; (3) environmental preferences; (4) user needs analysis; (5) participatory design techniques; and (6) post-occupancy evaluation. By the 1970s, appropriate technology and energy conservation could be added to the list. These can be separated from the others both because they came later and because they did not place the same reliance on user needs. Goals such as reducing automobile use or making energy-efficient buildings did not arise from consultation with occupants but from geopolitical realities. The task of the social scientist in the energy field was less to give people what they wanted than to change people's wants.

MAJOR AREAS

1. Human use of space. This work was inspired by zoologists and ethologists, such as Tinbergen and Hediger, who had studied the spatial needs of animals in their natural habitat.[3] It was found that most species of mammals in nature had territorial and spacing patterns related to vital activities of mating and food gathering. Heini Hediger, curator of the Zurich Zoo, found that if a captive animal were given too little, too much, or the wrong kinds of space, it would be likely to become listless, lose its body sheen, fail to reproduce, become ill, or die. Because of their tangible financial stake in keeping their animals fit and healthy, zookeepers embarked on a program to identify the spatial needs of various species. In his influential paper "Function as a Basis of Psychiatric Ward Design," Humphry Osmond declared that more was known about the spatial needs of captive animals than about the spatial needs of people.[4] On a larger scale, biologists were writing about the undesirable physiological and behavioral consequences of overpopulation.

Since virtually all other mammalian species have particular spatial needs, the logic seemed compelling that humans would have them also. These needs would necessarily be modified by environmental conditions, but their expression and the costs of adaptation could not be ignored. Social scientists borrowed terminology and methods from zoology since there was too little information available about human spatial needs. Eventually a vocabulary of human spatial concepts was developed. Edward Hall developed theories of proxemics based on observations of interpersonal distance in various nations.[5] Erving Goffman connected spacing to other nonverbal behaviors as part of a process of social regulation.[6] Roger Barker drew up plans for a behavioral ecology based on systematic observation of behavior over time.[7]

2. Awareness and environmental cognition. Kevin Lynch's *Image of the City* awakened interest in techniques for studying environmental imagery.[8] The *mental map* became a widely used research tool of city planners and geographers. A mental map involves people's conceptions of their own neighborhoods and significant places and objects. These maps were found to be spotty, selective, and highly personal documents that did not correspond to the way that planners thought people conceived of their environment.

The investigation of spatial imagery required new concepts and a new vocabulary, in addition to some techniques that did not depend so heavily on words. Philip Thiel has embarked on a quest for a vocabulary to describe human movement in space.[9] Christopher Alexander and his colleagues created a pattern language to link together design elements.[10] Other architects experimented with slides, videotapes, models, and computer drawings in place of blueprints and bubble diagrams, which had tended to confuse the public. Unlike traditional scale models or drawings, which tended to be polished, elegant, and often expensive from the standpoint of professional time, these new procedures were tentative and manipulable.[11] It was not so much a finished model that was presented to future residents as a kit of model parts that could be combined in different ways. The computer was brought in to create drawings showing how a façade would appear from different vantage points and distances. The uses of these techniques were not new in the design process. Architects for decades had been sitting down with clients and occasionally with prospective occupants and showing them drawings and models. What was new was the conscious commitment to use simulation procedures to obtain user input in a systematic manner and then to introduce this information into the planning process.

3. *Environmental preference.* The traditional view of experimental aesthetics had sought to identify the forms, shapes, and patterns that most people preferred or disliked.[12] It was assumed that there were identifiable properties in objects that would produce uniform judgments of beauty or ugliness, and given the choice, most people would choose the beautiful. Because this approach was unable to account for many of the unusual environmental choices made by people, a new strategy was tried that considered beauty to be one part of a larger number of environmental dimensions that included coherence, texture, identifiability, spaciousness, complexity, and mystery.[13] Tests were developed to measure individual differences in environmental preferences. People could be classified by the degree to which they liked to be in places that were ordered and predictable or exciting and novel. This approach had its widest application in landscape research. The U.S. Forest Service and the National Park Service supported studies intended to identify the outdoor preferences of diverse groups such as wilderness hikers and convenience campers.[14]

4. *User needs analysis.* The first task for social scientists in the design process was describing the needs and wants of environmental consumers. Questions tended to be specific to a particular project.

The city planner did not want to know about people in general but about a particular neighborhood in the path of a planned freeway. The interior designer did not want information about college students in general but about the particular undergraduates who would occupy a new residence hall. How would these students react to bunk beds, which provided extra floor space but required behavioral accommodations? What was the ideal number of occupants for a dormitory room? Being a consultant on user needs proved extremely frustrating for social scientists who had neither the information at their fingertips nor the time and resources to obtain it. Many of the traditional information-gathering procedures in the social sciences, such as experimentation and random sampling, were inappropriate for the kinds of questions that were being asked and for the time frame of design practice.

User needs analysis became associated with architectural programming, the listing of objectives served by a new building. It had been predicted that programming would create the niche for a new professional, half designer and half social scientist, who could systematically compile what people wanted and translate this information into a form usable to designers. With ingenuity and patience, the architectural/environmental needs of most user groups could be identified. Powell Lawton interviewed occupants of convalescent homes,[15] Frank Becker surveyed tenants of public housing projects,[16] Richard Farbstein asked inmates about jail conditions,[17] and Bonnie Kroll asked higher-grade mentally retarded patients about their environmental requirements and interviewed the staff about the needs of residents too feeble or uncommunicative to be approached directly.[18] The chief barriers to user needs analysis was not a shortage of methods or interviewers, but time, resources, and methods for translating the findings into design specifications.

5. *Participatory design.* Methods were needed to involve people directly in the planning process. Designers who had been trained to design *for* people had difficulty in designing *with* them. The new approach did not assume that everyone had equivalent experience, insight, or talent, but only that everyone's ideas and experiences had to be listened to with respect. The gardener had useful information for the landscape designer and the custodian for the interior designer. The occupants, both present and potential, could contribute important information if asked the right sort of questions in a supportive manner.

Planners explored the use of intensive group sessions with a heavy emphasis on emotional expression. Catharsis was considered necessary before the more rational design work could proceed. In

2

FIGURES 2–5 The earliest work in environmental psychology took place in institutional settings such as mental hospitals (Figures 2 and 3) and prisons (Figures 4 and 5) where the occupants had few environmental options.

3
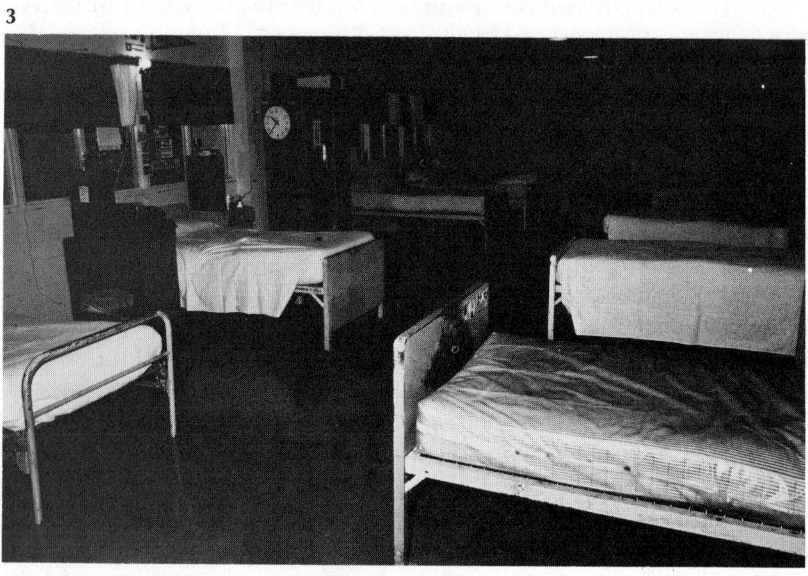

4

5

role-playing exercises such as the *charrette,* one person would play the part of a land developer, another an environmentalist, city official, construction worker, or a farmer who wanted to continue growing crops. They would sit around the table and discuss a proposed project from each individual's perspective. Midway through the discussion the players would switch parts. This provided insight into other views and hopefully laid the basis for compromise. The discussions often proved frustrating and time consuming, but the hoped-for reward was a greater involvement of people in the design process and a better fit between buildings and occupants.

6. Post-occupancy evaluation. Some designers were dissatisfied with the constant need to reinvent the wheel, which often turned out to be a square, lopsided, or even wrong-sized wheel. Firms hired to design a library or an airport would discuss the matter with the clients, visit a few similar buildings, read whatever was available, and then do the best they could. There was not a body of information available on past projects that could be applied to new construction. The architect would be heavily involved in the planning and construction stages, but disappear by the time a building was completed, except for a perfunctory return visit to do the fine tuning. This provided little opportunity to learn how a project worked in practice or for the profession to move from an intuitive and subjective problem-solving approach to an empirical level in which new projects were built on the results of past projects in some systematic manner. A firm might go on building the same kind of bank in six cities without ever making a systematic attempt to find out how employees or customers responded to particular features. When firms did attempt to determine how a building worked in practice, the information was often proprietary and unavailable to competitors.

Post-occupancy evaluation was developed as a means of dealing with these issues. It involved looking closely at completed buildings to see how they worked in practice. There was no limit to the number of aspects that could be examined, but they always included the level of occupant satisfaction. Buildings were no longer to be considered for awards by a remote committee of judges viewing glossy photographs taken from odd angles using special lenses and fancy filters. Systematic post-occupancy evaluation required a commitment of professional time and resources, support and cooperation from the client or owner, methods for making and comparing standardized evaluations, and a feed-forward process that intersected with the construction. Social scientists were called upon to provide instruments and methods for gauging satisfaction levels among oc-

FIGURE 6 Sociofugal space. Narrow aisles make it difficult for supermarket shoppers to converse.

FIGURE 7 Sociopetal space. Layout and social organization of the West Allis (WI) Farmers' Market encourages interaction.

cupants. They were also called upon to do the actual surveys. Such tasks required modification of the research model under which most social scientists had been trained.

Appropriate technology was not a concern in the early liaison between design and the social sciences. It came later with the realization of present and future energy shortages. Many of the practices of the previous decade were rejected as wasteful and inhumane. Buildings that turned their back on the neighborhood also tended to reject local materials, culture, and the landscape. Ian McHarg emphasized the importance of designing with nature.[19] Inoperable windows and centralized control of utilities not only squandered valuable resources but oppressed the occupants. The renewed emphasis on decentralization and local control in appropriate technology parallels the social designer's values of participation and user input. People can participate more fully in small face-to-face groups than in large impersonal organizations.

FROM CONCERN TO PRACTICE

The various contributions of behavioral scientists to the design process are diagrammed in Figure 8. This shows how the different activities intersect with practice. Some of the problems that have arisen during collaboration between architects and social scientists have resulted from ambiguity about which role was being played or when an activity was likely to be useful; for example, the architect hired a psychologist as a consultant while the psychologist expected to do research; or people undertook evaluations of existing buildings and wondered why the information was not being used in new construction.

The design of a building proceeds through various stages, including planning, financing, programming, and working drawings, through construction and beyond. Behavioral science input will most likely occur at the programming stage through needs analysis or consultation, and later during a post-occupancy evaluation (POE). Behavioral scientists can also play a role in the preparation of the Environmental Impact Statement, particularly in discussing the effects of a new project upon the social life of a neighborhood. On other projects a social scientist may help increase occupant awareness regarding a new project and its implications. The social scientists' role may go beyond awareness to organization and political action, although there is little reason to suppose that they are better suited to these activities than other individuals. Neither consultation nor post-occupancy evaluation is given its own

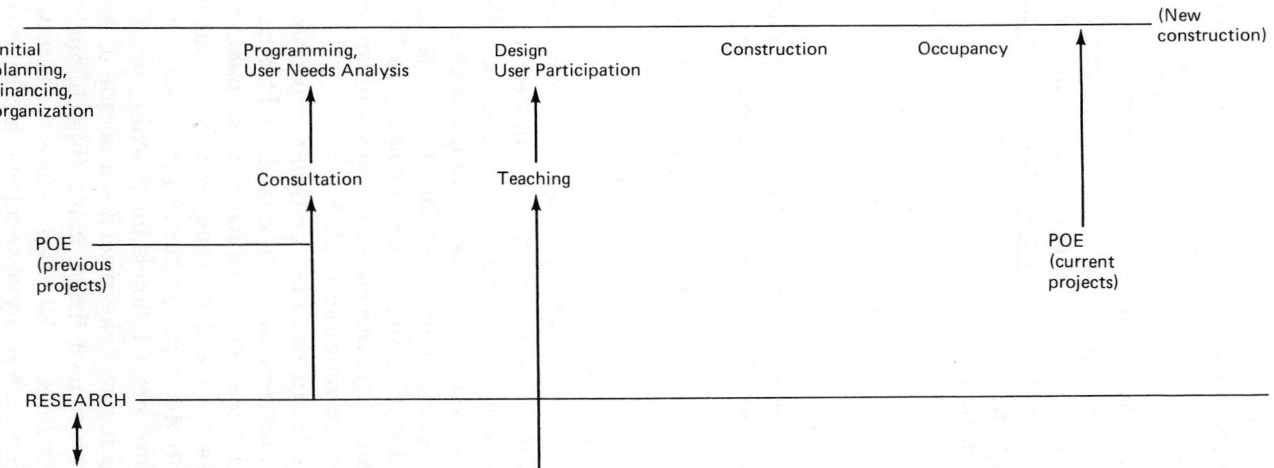

FIGURE 8 How behavioral science activities intersected with design practice.

time line in Figure 8 since they are tied to the temporal and fiscal coordinates of design practice. Research and theory are separate activities that continue beyond single projects. Theory does not intersect design practice directly, but rather affects it through research, which enters design practice through consultation. There are no structural barriers to a social scientist's being engaged in more than one activity, for example, a theorist's becoming a design consultant or a researcher's evaluating an occupied building. Expanding one's role in this manner requires an acceptance of different timetables, methods, and expectations regarding the likelihood of implementations of ideas into practice.

Consultation and needs analysis occur at the front end of a project. Psychologists were first brought into the design process as consultants. Once it was found that they did not have the necessary information at their fingertips, the value of undertaking systematic needs assessment surveys became apparent. There is good likelihood that *some* of the material from the needs analysis will be incorporated in the solution. However, the results of a needs analysis or consultation are not likely to be published or known outside a specific project.

As it is presently used, the evaluation can be expected to have little impact on the building being examined, which is already completed, and the budget for construction of new structures or modification of existing ones spent. For a post-occupancy evaluation to influence new construction, a feed-forward model to new buildings of the same or related type is required. POE is largely an empirical approach characterized by eclecticism in theory and methods, but there is no inherent disadvantage in an evaluator's having a theoretical perspective, for example, looking at neighborhoods from the standpoint of Durkheim's *anomie*[20] or Newman's *defensible space*.[21] Although theories may be useful in guiding observations, they are not required in POE.

Research can have a significant impact on design theory, but its effects upon practice will be mediated through education and consultation. Basic studies are likely to be published in academic journals where they will be read by other academics. Schools of architecture provide a means for bringing research findings to the attention of *students*. Channels for reaching practitioners are less obvious. Since it may take students a decade or longer to become principals in their own firms, using this channel for influencing practice may take 10 to 20 years before the results are seen. Just when researchers are ready to conclude that their work has had no impact, a generation of designers exposed to social science teaching and research will begin making management decisions.

Theory can influence practice in a number of ways. One route is through research that confirms or supports the theory before it is applied. Good ideas can be exceedingly important in guiding research and the education of students. Barker's behavior setting theory was not intended to influence practice directly, but it has had a major long-range impact on research.[22] Robert Bechtel adapted the behavior setting approach for use in housing projects and won the AIA research award for his efforts.[23] Theory can also take a shortcut through practice—circumventing research. Many fields without a strong research tradition, such as architecture and design, are susceptible to catchy images that may not have a great deal of empirical support. Office landscaping came into design for a variety of extraneous reasons, some of which had little to do with the economic advantages of flexibility. The high-rise public housing buildings surrounded by lush green spaces had great visual appeal but little empirical support when they swept the western world after the Second World War. In an ideal world, theory should be followed by research before it influences practice, but in a world in which a catchy phrase may have instant appeal, the research may come later and fail to support the theory that has already been set into concrete.

Although Figure 8 keeps separate consultation from research and post-occupancy evaluation, these activities are not so clearly demarcated in real life. There are POEs that have been guided by theory and expanded into research projects. Distinctions and definitions are needed so long as people realize that in practice they are not nearly as discrete as they appear on paper. Critic, writer, and poet Paul Goodman, whose interests spanned both design and psychology, was critical of attempts to create major upsets in systems and labeled himself a "neolithic conservative." He advocated tinkering with institutions, and making minor improvements rather than major upheavals. He viewed the role of the behavioral scientist as being like that of the literary critic. "A literary critic doesn't seek to produce a poem," Goodman wrote, "rather he takes an ongoing situation and says 'It can run a little more smoothly if we fix this little piece here and fix that little piece there.' "[24] Behavioral scientists should come across as humanist critics rather than as a priori or empirical systems builders. This has been called the politics of muddle. It requires that the social scientist and the designer have big ears and listen to what other people say. This is the opposite of top-down planning, in which policy makers are guided by abstract notions and grand schemes. There will be times for bold new visions of the future, as in the case of space travel, but we should be careful about imposing these on other people. There is some indication that massive skyscrapers, which may be as high as the architectural profession is able to go in space travel, have many undesirable social consequences. Improving what exists may be a useful and valid role for social scientists in the design process. When an architect comes up with a bold new scheme based on a personal image and is able to find a sponsor, the role of the social scientist may be limited to documentation, fine tuning, and dissemination. Such activities are congenial to the training and skills of many social scientists. Often this means coming in at the end of projects and attempting to reconstruct what had gone on earlier. Mark Francis, Lisa Cashdan, and Lynn Paxson conducted case studies of neighborhood open spaces converted into gardens, mini-parks, and playing fields in New York City.[25] The researchers were not involved in the early stages of the open space development, but came in afterwards to document what had happened and also to make suggestions as to how each site could be improved. This commitment to change as part of an evaluation plan follows the action research model pioneered by Kurt Lewin.[26]

TRAINING OF SOCIAL DESIGNERS

Certain skills are more important in social design than in traditional design practice.

1. Methods to determine how people are affected by the built environment. The social designer needs to know something about observational procedures, interview and questionnaire methods, photography (how to include people in the pictures) and case studies of both important and mundane buildings.

Zeisel and Sommer and Sommer provide an introduction to these techniques.[27] Hands-on experience is required before proficiency is obtained. One can read books and articles about behavioral mapping, but until one actually tries to chart people in space, one cannot fully comprehend the benefits and the shortcomings of the method. The social designer has a bag of these tricks available depending upon the nature of the setting, the activities, and the occupants. Attention must be given to the cost-effectiveness of each approach. Timing is always a crucial consideration. There is no point in seeking a slightly more valid method if the data will arrive too late to be used.

2. Techniques for involving users in planning decisions. There are many differences between working with a single client face to face and working with a group of tenants or with a community. Talking is as much a part of the social designer's job as drawing and writing. Various techniques have been developed for increasing group participation, including workshops, charrettes, simulation exercises, Delphi techniques, and so on. Graphic presentation is essential both for showing people design alternatives and for allowing their views to intersect with traditional design approaches which involve sketches, models, and drawings.

3. *Method for educating people to get more satisfaction from the built environment.* Much of the work of the social designer involves settings whose occupants are turned off to their surroundings. The first task will be to establish connections between people and the environment. It may be desirable to provide occupants with written instructions showing how to make the best use of a building in order to do their jobs effectively, save energy, and increase personal comfort.

4. *Communication skills that cross professional, social class, and language barriers.* These are especially important when a project involves residents who are of a cultural background different from that of the client or the designer. Specific measures will be needed to overcome such cultural barriers. Social scientists and designers are not immune from speaking in their own professional jargon. Some translation may be necessary to present their recommendations so that they are understandable to outsiders. For me personally, one of the most difficult languages in planning sessions is bureaucratic speech, for example, "There is money available under a 176 grant which replaces the 235 program but we'll have to file an EIR with EPA."

5. *Archival research.* No matter how unusual the project, there is always some precedent available. There is no such thing as a totally new building. The social designer must know how to use the available information resources and how to contact firms, agencies, and individuals through correspondence and telephone to find out what they have done. The availability of secondary sources, such as state-of-the-art volumes in specialty areas, makes this task easier. The social designer will have to put this information into a form that is usable to practitioners. Often this will mean translating general statements into design specifications.

There are impressive information resources available in libraries. However, too many design students make more use of the library slide collection than of the book collection. I have no objection to the enlargement of a student's image banks, but there is a wealth of valuable printed material available. I would strongly advocate that library exercises be a part of design education. Students might be asked, for example, to present a report on laundromat design, color in carpeting, or theatrical lighting. The assignment would require the student to sift through a lot of material quickly and come up with the best state-of-the-art information. The task is not to come up with a new design—that comes later—but to find out what has been done before on the topic. The report should include references. The student who missed key sources would be required to go back and locate them. Even a brief literature review can have an excellent cost-benefit ratio. It is embarrassing for a firm to discover, halfway into a project, that it has been trying to solve a problem that others have already solved. To display unfamiliarity with the important work of others is a sure prescription for losing credibility with a client.

All of these skills also have a place in traditional design education, even though they are especially useful in studying people-place relationships. Perhaps the single most important addition to existing curricula for teaching students to respect the diversity and range of occupant opinion is the post-occupancy evaluation. Conducting a POE provides young designers with a way of verifying their own preconceptions about people's responses. I favor a requirement that all planning and architecture students evaluate at least one setting during their academic training. This might be anything from a church to a factory, and the evaluation would include physical measures of air circulation, temperature, lighting, and energy costs, as well as the activities and attitudes of the occupants, owners, managers, and custodians. Rather than creating special courses in building evaluation, which would be isolated from the main curriculum, it would be preferable to include the evaluation in senior studio courses. As part of a course assignment to design a particular type of structure, the student could be required to systematically evaluate an example of the building type on which the class is working. The student who has evaluated a building never sees that building in the same way again. Just as a historical analysis or a photographic study of a building can change the way the structure is seen, a POE does this in terms of deepening the evaluator's understanding of people-place relationships.

THEORETICAL INFLUENCES

A good theory can be extraordinarily practical in identifying what is important and how to get at it. It saves time and energy if one can limit the predicted range of consequences without always having to start from ground zero. Social design theories can be used to identify the social consequences of proposed solutions early in the planning process, when various alternatives are still being generated, thus helping to determine on a rational basis the appropriateness of proposed alternatives for different goals and objectives. Theory can also act as a source of design objectives that can guide the search for appropriate solutions and can indicate those issues on which no predictions can be made, thus making explicit the need for research.

The major theoretical influences upon social design came from ecology and humanistic psychology. The cardinal assumption of ecological theory is interdependence—everything is connected, and a change in any aspect will reverberate throughout a system. The various levels within both organismic and environmental systems will develop, flourish, and decline in predictable ways, although not necessarily in the same ways. The environment is conceived of in multidimensional dynamic terms, and the focus of analysis generally is upon interrelations among people and their surroundings (human ecology) rather than on the linkages between single stimuli and behavioral responses.[1] Applying this notion of interdependency to people and places is not easy. Many people are overwhelmed by the implications of unbounded systems, not knowing where to start or finish if everything is connected and there are no clear beginnings and ends. It is difficult to put a fixed date on either the start of something as tangible as a building or as intangible as a planning process. The first glimmer of thinking about a new structure may have occurred when the occupants first moved into its predecessor and found it too small. Formal discussion would not start until several years later, when a suitable site was obtained. Then financing would have to be arranged, an architect hired, and the preliminary plans submitted and approved. Construction would proceed and continue even after the client moved in. Such a structure is never completed in any final sense, since there is always work to be done. Change and flux characterize buildings as they do everything else. Even as I write about a building, it is changing. The ecological perspective accepts this kind of fluidity and attempts to introduce taps into the system at discrete points as a means of studying growth and development. Fortunately, there is usually a coherent core within all the change that provides shared meanings and makes possible discussion about things in flux.

Environmental psychology borrowed its methods more from the natural sciences than from the physical sciences. The ambivalence of environmental researchers to laboratory experimentation was well expressed by David Canter in his book *The Psychology of Place:*

> *In the text I had eschewed, in the main, any reference to studies performed within the major psychological rubric, the laboratory experiment. This was not as much a deliberate policy as the desire to deal with research clearly and directly related to the experience of the environment. By their very nature, laboratories lead to an abstraction of particular stimuli from their natural habitat.*[2]

The experimental method is an efficient means of separating out causal influences. It is much less satisfactory, however, for putting things together and understanding how they work in the natural world. The laboratory is a splendid place for learning how objects, colors, or sounds are perceived in the laboratory. It is not very useful for learning how things are perceived in the city, yet there are situations where a researcher will want to create laboratory simulation of something too difficult to find or study in the outside world. Photographic simulation is an economical approach to exploring how people respond to a wide range of forms, colors, or textures. What distinguishes the environmental psychologist from more traditional perception researchers is that the environmental researcher thinks first of a study in the outside world and only goes into the laboratory when it seems necessary, while the more traditional psychologist operates in reverse order.

The second major theoretical influence on social design was humanistic psychology, which itself had arisen from an earlier group dynamics movement. This was a body of theory and speculation associated with writers such as Carl Rogers, Abraham Maslow, Harry Stack Sullivan, and Gardner Murphy. It emphasized not the clinic, which had been the concern of psychoanalysts, or the laboratory, which is so dear to the hearts of behaviorists, but people developing and responding to an outside environment. Kurt Lewin attempted to diagram "life space" as it was impinged upon by outside forces.[3] Participatory design methods came out of the group dynamics approach pioneered by Lewin and his coworkers. Humanistic psychology emphasized the legitimacy of individual experience and the possibilities of personal growth. It represented an optimistic outlook in contrast to its more mechanistic and pessimistic predecessors, psychoanalysis and behaviorism. Phenomenological analysis was an important tool for studying experience. Rather than reducing views of the world to prepared concepts and categories, the phenomenologist attempts to understand the world in the terms that people themselves use. The work of Gaston Bachelard, Claire Cooper-Marcus, and Perla Korosec-Serfaty illustrates the application of this approach to architecture. Environmental autobiography was one means of making explicit one's experiences with a place by raising personal experience to a level of consciousness and making it available to designers for their use.[4]

The humanists' concern with existential themes of loneliness and alienation meshed with the social design objective of increasing people's connections to the environment. The psychological process used to counteract alienation from buildings was *ego involvement*—being involved with something changes one's experience of it. Playing even a small part in selecting furniture or planning a room layout will alter the participant's feeling toward that space. Different degrees of personal involvement with buildings could be noted, from no involvement, which is characteristic of institutions such as hospitals and prisons, to total involvement, as in the case of a house designed, constructed, and furnished by the eventual occupant. The phenomenological methods of humanistic psychology were more appropriate for studying issues such as alienation and involvement than were experimental approaches. Apart from this use of phenomenological analysis, which remains strong in Europe, the influence of humanistic psychology upon design waned as its methods and rhetoric became excessively preoccupied with self-improvement (critics called it narcissism), and it lost interest in the outside world. However, at the beginning of social design, humanistic psychology played an important role in expanding architects' ideas of the human potential and providing methods for studying personal experience different from the survey techniques typically used.

Some attempts were made to build bridges between environmental psychology and behaviorism. This was a natural association, since the behaviorism pioneered by John B. Watson and later modified by B. F. Skinner was known as *environmentalism*. Environmental psychology and behaviorism both emphasized external causes of behavior as distinct from internal forces such as heredity, personality, and social attitudes. Like behavior modification, environmental psychology is usually considered to be an applied field. Two of the best known practitioners of behavioral modification, Harold Cohen and Israel Goldiamond, had been students at the Chicago

School of Design in the late 1940s. On the other side of the collaboration, Buckminster Fuller, the noted futurist designer, was a major consultant to the Institute for Behavioral Research, one of the most active organizations in the field of behavior modification.[5]

The interests of behaviorists and environmental psychologists complemented each other in important ways. Much of the research of behaviorists has been concerned with the effects of behavior upon the environment. Cone and Hayes distinguish between two major classes of behavior toward the environment: protective and destructive.[6] Protective responses such as recycling, using public transportation, buying energy-efficient appliances, and bicycling, improve environmental quality. A major goal of environmental researchers is to find ways to strengthen these activities while at the same time reducing such environmentally destructive behaviors as vandalism, littering, and wasteful use of resources. Experiments have shown that the selective use of rewards reduced the amount of litter inside buildings, reduced unwanted noise, increased the use of public transportation, and helped promote energy conservation.[7]

Despite the similarities, there are important differences that have kept the two fields apart. Behavior modification was developed in the laboratory while environmental psychology developed in the outside world. Behaviorists placed major or exclusive emphasis on measurable behavior change, while environmental researchers frequently used subjective statements of comfort, preference, or satisfaction. Behaviorists are committed to the improvement of individuals through changes in the payoff system within the environment (that is, reinforcing socially desired behaviors) while environmental psychologists are committed to the improvement of physical settings with the expectations that this will affect the quality of life in a positive way. Many of those who practice behavior modification regard themselves as therapists, while this is not the case with environmental psychologists. The behaviorist starts out with specific goals (for example, the reduction of litter or vandalism) and then uses an existing technology for achieving these goals. The social designer spends more time and effort helping groups define their environmental objectives and evolve methods for attaining them.

B. F. Skinner, patriarch of behavioral psychology, recently made an autobiographical statement on methods of coping with failing memory and other diminished intellectual powers that may come with old age.[8] Skinner's solution was to create a stimulating environment for himself, devising little memory tricks and working fewer hours. A great deal of what is considered aging is not simply a biological process, but a change in the physical and social environment. Vision, hearing, and taste fade, and the intensity of stimulation is reduced, thus making the elderly more bored, discouraged, and depressed. To counter this, information coming in from the environment can be sharpened and enhanced. Good lighting and proper glasses can increase the value of visual information. Spicier foods and sauces can perk up otherwise dull meals. When behavioristic psychologists talk like this, the line between them and other environmental psychologists disappears.

The liaison between design and social science was expected to enrich theory in both fields. Most architectural theory had dealt with buildings apart from people, and most psychological theories dealt with the human psyche separately from the environment. Now environmental psychology was advocating theories focused upon people-place relationships. Friendship was seen not as an abstract quality, but as something that occurs between people in specific settings. What is there in a place that encourages conversation and mutual assistance? The older concerns of social psychology were made situation-specific. Some existing psychological theories such as Berlyne's notions of stimulus complexity[9] and Gibson's theories of vision[10] were applied to environmental problems. New concepts were also developed, such as Osmond's theory of sociofugal spaces.[11] Certain types of buildings, such as airports, classrooms, and supermarkets seemed to be designed to keep people from interacting (see Example A). The defensible space concept proposed by Oscar Newman was helpful in pinpointing aspects of buildings that inhibit crime.[12] Newman found that low-rise public housing projects, in which residents could identify with individual buildings and had good surveillance of the surrounding areas, have lower crime and vandalism rates than high-rise projects that have many areas, which belong to no one in particular, hidden from public view (see Example B). On a larger environmental scale, Lynch proposed the city image to explain how people conceived of their immediate environment.[13] Mental mapping techniques allowed quantitative analysis and the comparison of images of different groups of people.

Theory is particularly important in environmental psychology because of the variety and complexity of the places studied. It provides a way of finding commonality among different settings used for different purposes. At London's Bartlett School of Architecture, the two most emphasized areas of psychology were space perception and small group behavior. The approach was both to study the basic findings in the area and to connect theory to the student's own life and future work as an architect.[14] Not all design research will contribute to theory, of course. If all the post-occupancy evaluations of hospitals, banks, and cafeterias were compiled, they would make only a minuscule contribution to theory. The authors of such documents were trying to be useful to planners and believed that a general discussion of aesthetics or privacy would be a distraction.

Theorists such as Alexander, Altman, Barker, Ittelson, Thiel, and Wohlwill have tried to solve the puzzles that challenged the early Greek philosophers. The controversy of free will versus determinism was recast as the extent to which motivation was internally or externally caused. The competing models of people and the environment bore a remarkable likeness to the earlier body-mind theories known as monism, dualism, and parallelism. Instead of asking whether body and mind were separate or together, the environmental theorists debated whether people and the environment were a single inseparable unit (monism), two independent entities (dualism), or whether they operated on separate but parallel planes (parallelism). The long-range effectiveness of all those who deal with people-place relationships will depend upon the efforts of theorists who can jump across areas, see relationships, and pull together disparate findings.

A major contribution of the social design movement has been the broadening of acceptable research areas. Twenty years ago the emphasis in landscape architecture was on greenery, topography, and other physical characteristics of outdoor spaces. It would have been unusual for a landscape student to study how people space themselves in parks or plazas. Today landscape students are not only studying these topics, but also people's responses to different types of plants and garden layouts. There is recognition that consumer acceptance is necessary if water-conserving plants are to be used in the public environment. There is also lively discussion about why so many city parks are underutilized and unloved by nearby residents,[15] and how residents are taking action to change public open spaces to better fit their needs. The social design movement laid the groundwork for the development of landscape theories that include people-land and people-plant relationships.

PROBLEMS THAT DEVELOPED

Some of the things that were included under the heading of social design did not fit together. The idea that architects might profit from introductory psychology courses or that social scientists should take studio courses was tried a few times and then was quietly dropped. It probably had some value in general education but hardly qualified as social design. Introductory psychology courses were intended for liberal arts undergraduates and contained little information useful to designers. On the other side, studio courses lacked the intellectual rigor necessary to challenge liberal arts students who wanted to know why rather than how things should be done. Most liberal arts students lacked the graphic and visual skills needed for effective communication in design.

The hope that an experimental science could be developed to study occupied buildings was quickly dashed. People, those fickle and inconsiderate creatures, spoil experiments by changing their environments to suit their needs. Two Canadian researchers failed in their attempt to compare the summer comfort conditions in two occupied houses that used different construction methods because the people in the buildings behaved so differently that all the differences attributable to physical construction were effectively masked.[16] The main feature in the downfall of the experiment was the uncontrolled opening and closing of windows. It is true that this can be experimentally controlled by making windows inoperable, but how could these results be applied to real people living in real summer cottages? In another case, two houses were fitted with aluminum windows and frames and observed over the course of a winter. Tenants in one house reported no difficulties with the windows. They did, however, ventilate the house extensively by opening windows, and they dried all their wash outdoors, making the indoor humidity so low as to cause no condensation on the window frames. The tenants in the second house ended up with a coating of as much as one inch of ice on the warm side of the window sills, due to the fact that the wash was hung indoors and the windows were never opened, thus maintaining a high moisture content in the house. These incidents illustrate some of the problems in the experimental study of occupied buildings. Predictions cannot be made about the effectiveness of a building without knowing how it is to be used and for what purposes. Such incidents suggest the value of an *empirical,* as distinguished from an *experimental,* building science. The former takes into account the different ways in which buildings will be used by different groups of people, whereas an experimental science tends to conceive of buildings in isolation from any occupants.

What did all this mean for someone sitting at a drafting table? Not very much, but I don't think that this is the right question. The image of drafting tables locates the scene in the architect's office. The thrust of social design was to get architects into neighborhoods and to get clients concerned about users of their buildings and open spaces. Also, the important work in social design occurred before a project reached the drawing boards. It involved a consultative process that went on prior to the designer's taking a pencil to a sketch pad.

Any movement that develops rapidly will lack the internal controls to keep all of its activities within acceptable bounds. It will likely "go too far" without its being noticed by supporters who attribute resistance to conservatism, ignorance, or personality conflicts. Social design went through its infancy and adolescence quickly. In the 1960s the time was ripe for a message of participation and user input. Architecture had itself "gone too far" in neglecting user needs. The *Fountainhead* ideal of the Master Designer who is heedless of occupant views and the Master Planner who excludes neighborhood input gave rise to their own antithesis in the form of social design.

There were problems and irritations in the new movement. The consulting process occasionally dragged on interminably as user groups with conflicting goals demanded to have their views heard and accepted. Participation and input became buzzwords with more rhetoric than substance. Survey data occasionally became an excuse for neglecting aesthetics, and psychobabble substituted for critical judgment. Some planners interpreted "community participation" to mean design by majority vote. Occupants were asked questions that they could not answer and this became an indictment of the entire approach. When done without feeling, consultation became a formality that left everyone dissatisfied with the outcome. Many of the hopes of those who initially perceived the value of user consultation were quickly dashed by the time and emotional drain of genuine dialogue. A single meeting between designers and a tenants' committee or neighborhood association would identify more problems than it could solve.

There was some legitimacy to all these criticisms, but there were alternatives that involved changing the design process to accommodate user input. If residents were uninformed, or could not understand the designer's terminology, models or sketches could be used and options explained. The solution was not to bring people into the existing design process in a token manner but to alter the design process to provide a place for informed occupant opinion. Mercifully, the effects of the mistakes were minimal and cluttered up the journals more than they did the landscape. Social design did not become identified with a particular style. When local residents were included in the planning process, they did not automatically demand yurts, domes, and teepees as some critics had feared, but rather humane, nonoppressive buildings with natural light, windows that opened, ample greenery, the ability to personalize their spaces, and materials and forms connected to the surrounding neighborhoods and landscape.

EXAMPLES

A. The Lonely Supermarket Shopper: The Theory of Sociofugal Space

Based on his research into mental hospital architecture, psychiatrist Humphry Osmond described buildings whose layout actively discouraged interaction as *sociofugal.*[17] These structures are regarded by their occupants as cold, stark, institutional, and resistant to personalization or change. They can be contrasted with *sociopetal* buildings intended to bring people together, which embody warm colors, absorbent surfaces, movable furnishings, and allow numerous possibilities for personalization and modification. Settings can be ranked by their occupants as to the degree to which they are sociofugal or sociopetal.

One of the most common sociofugal settings is the modern supermarket. It almost seems to be deliberately designed to keep people separate from each other and to focus attention exclusively on the products. Shopping in supermarkets today is not regarded as fun. When the first "supers" opened in the 1930s, the experience of selecting items directly from the shelves was exciting and enjoyable. One writer observed that, "Housewives enjoyed visiting the markets for the circusy, bazaar atmosphere which prevailed, and provided release for the suppressed emotions piled up within many women by the dreary monotony of Depression days."[18] Shoppers could exercise more control over the situation than they could in small stores where access to the products was through a store clerk or the owner. The realization of the self-service ideal has made the stores more sociofugal. Two Japanese journalists commented that the sterility and standardization of the American supermarket "takes away the social pleasures of shopping,"[19] and greengrocer Joe Carcione speaks of "impersonal supermarket merchandising."[20] Bloom and Greyser believe that the depersonalization of shopping was one factor that contributed to the rise of the consumer movement in the 1960s.[21]

Like other sociofugal buildings, the supermarket is disconnected from its neighborhood and region. The only sense of place provided to the customer is being inside a supermarket. If one were to kidnap, blindfold, and confine people inside supermarkets in cities around the United States, it is doubtful that many could determine their location from any aspect of the store's interior. Nor would the exterior provide many clues, especially in the larger chains that capitalize upon a national image.

From an aesthetic standpoint, the supermarket has improved considerably from the time when Mike Cullen opened the first of his "price wreckers" in an abandoned garage in Jamaica, New York, using only pine board tables with cases of canned foods cut open so that shoppers could serve themselves. Both the merchandise and the surroundings were known as "cheapies" since the floors lacked covering, partitions were torn out, counters and display fixtures were made of rough pine boards, and the stores were located in low-rent districts on the fringes of thickly populated areas.[22] As the supermarket concept took hold and new stores were built, more attention was given to the customer's comfort and convenience. Lighting was improved, open tables were replaced by cupboards, floor covering was added, and color was used to express a store theme. However this attention to improved aesthetics did not improve the social atmosphere. While the surroundings were made more attractive, they also became less friendly. New designs removed employees and management from the selling areas and made it difficult for customers to interact.

Documentation of the social atmosphere was made through interaction counts in supermarkets in 15 California cities. Similar counts were made in farmers' markets and co-op stores, two alternative retail outlets reminiscent of the time when the sale of food was a local enterprise. For most supermarket customers, the only verbal contact with another person was a perfunctory interaction with the checkout clerk. A supermarket customer had less than a one-in-ten chance of a social contact with another customer during a single shopping trip. By contrast, a farmers' market customer had a two-in-three likelihood of a social contact with another customer.[23] Similar results were found in the comparisons between commercial supermarkets and member-owned cooperative stores. Co-op members enjoyed the shopping experience more than did supermarket patrons.[24] The co-ops were found to be friendlier places than the supermarkets, as measured both in customer ratings and counts of actual conversations taking place.[25]

The factors responsible for the low level of interaction in supermarkets are both architectural and organizational. The basis of the modern supermarket is self-service. The customer who comes upon a clerk stacking cans or stamping prices is likely to feel apologetic about bothering this busy person. Although the clerk will be polite and helpful, it is clear to both that the clerk's primary duty is servicing the merchandise rather than the customers. Management is generally located in a remote area out of the main traffic flow. The only employee that the customer will encounter is the checkout clerk under conditions not likely to provoke more than a brief encounter.

While the existing pattern of staff organization is primarily responsible for the low level of interaction between employees and customers, it cannot explain the low level of interaction among customers. To understand this, we have to examine the physical layout, which provides no places where conversation can take place. People wheeling carts down the aisles following a main traffic flow are not likely to meet those who enter the store much earlier or later. The main opportunities for the customer to encounter friends will occur in the minor aisles where the traffic flow is less predictable. However, meeting a friend or neighbor in a narrow aisle is not likely to produce a conversation if there is no place to stop and chat. It is also difficult for a customer to make a U-turn in a crowded aisle to join a friend, and there is no way to walk with someone side-by-side down a narrow aisle. It would be equally frustrating to attempt a conversation in a busy store wheeling a wagon in front of or behind someone else's wagon. The most likely outcome is that customers restrict supermarket meetings to brief perfunctory exchanges. The lack of opportunity for satisfying conversation is one reason why so many customers shop alone. In counts made among 900 supermarket shoppers in one city, 84 percent came to the store alone.[26] There is no reason to have someone else along if there is no opportunity to talk with him or her.

A good theory ties together research and findings from a variety of different settings. It allows underlying similarities to be seen in spite of superficial differences. Viewing the supermarket as an instance of sociofugal architecture helps connect its physical layout and social organization to other institutional buildings such as airports, schools, prisons, hospitals, and so on. The theory allows for predictions regarding common behavior patterns found in settings that alienate people, for example, withdrawal, frustration, vandalism, and so on, and also the specification of remedies based on loosening up the physical and social system to create opportunities for personalization. A combination of physical and social measures must be used to combat desocialization in the supermarket. To change the physical layout to make employees visually accessible to customers, without redefining employee roles, will do little more than increase frustration levels on all sides. Correspondingly, to change employee roles but leave the unfriendly physical layout intact will provide little space or opportunity for employees to conveniently and efficiently assist customers. The value of the social design approach, as exemplified in the theory of sociofugal space, is the focus of attention upon people-place relationships as a conceptual unity.

B. Locking the Bathroom Door: Theory of Defensible Space

Large public housing projects sprang up like mushrooms throughout the United States and much of Europe following the Second World War. The architects who designed them were motivated by humanitarian principles and were heavily influenced by Le Corbusier's visions of the radiant city—tall sparkling spires set amidst parklike settings where the occupants could relax, breathe, and enjoy visual respite.[27] By concentrating a large number of people in a few tall towers, space on the ground could be preserved for parks, playgrounds, and gardens. This image turned into a nightmare when applied to public housing.

Rates of crime and vandalism were higher in large anonymous towers than they were in nearby low-rise walkup apartment buildings, even though the populations residing in the two types of buildings were very similar in socioeconomic characteristics.[28] Surprisingly, the low-rise buildings, because they were close together, could be built to about the same density as the high-rise structures. Oscar Newman attributed the increased crime to the destructive effects of the tall buildings upon the social life of the occupants.[29] The towers impeded any possibility of territorial definition or self-defense by the residents. The structures were so large that people did not know who belonged there. The elevators, stairwells, and the outside areas were dangerous places, hidden from public view.

Newman found that the best and least expensive medium-density housing were three-story walkups that could be built up to a density of 50 units per acre. They were less costly per square foot than either high-rise or row houses. The walkups did not require elevators, garbage chutes, or any of the emergency exits and elaborate fireproofing required in high-rise construction. In the smaller structures people could psychologically identify with particular buildings, visually survey the immediate area, and thus regulate children's play outside and challenge strangers who did not seem to belong inside. Occupants of the small buildings were willing to call the police if this were necessary. In the large buildings tenants were unwilling to call police since they were unsure about who had a legitimate reason for being there, and also because police were reluctant to come, and seemed uncomfortable in the large anonymous spaces with many alcoves, too many exits and entrances to control, and hidden places for snipers.

Newman developed his theory of defensible space out of these observations. The theory identified those characteristics of buildings that enhanced the ability of residents to protect themselves, thus drawing upon the existing protective desires of the occupants rather than upon outside force such as the police. Good defensible space makes it easy for people to see what is going on, challenge intruders, and take other appropriate action. The two major components of defensible space are surveillance and territoriality. Surveillance refers to the ability of occupants to see what is going on in and around the residences, to become familiar with their neighbors, and to keep track of suspicious activities. Good surveillance is achieved by proper positioning of windows with respect to entrances, parking lots, and grassy areas. On existing projects where faulty design created areas hidden from public view, high-technology solutions such as alarms or video cameras may be substituted for the human presence. These are, however, considered a less desirable alternative than the presumed presence of people who live in the project.

The occupants' feelings of territoriality are enhanced through real or symbolic barriers that mark areas as belonging to particular apartments or buildings. Strangers can be challenged when they enter marked space with a polite "Can I help you?" or with firmer language, if necessary. Real barriers include hedges, fences, and gates. Symbolic barriers would be decorative trim or plantings associated with particular entrances, or changes in sidewalk texture around patios or doorways. Identifying areas with particular residential units whose occupants have visual control over them develops proprietary attitudes. This enables the tenants to be the prime agents in maintaining order. Buildings with poor defensible space (large projects, buildings more than seven stories tall, superblocks closed to city traffic, long double-loaded corridors, and outside areas with no relationship to particular buildings) made it impossible for tenants to know one another or know what was going on in the surrounding area. This encouraged people not to intervene and thereby allowed crimes to happen.

Other researchers have extended Newman's findings to nonresidential settings such as commercial buildings, streets, and parks.[30] Good defensible space in these settings means that people who live nearby must take a proprietary interest in the public environment. Instead of closing off schools, hospitals, and other public buildings from neighborhoods, thus creating fortress-like, unfriendly structures, the idea is to design them to fit into neighborhoods. This is accomplished by developing multiple uses for buildings, such as opening schools in the evening as community centers, allowing concerts to be held in the parks, increasing the external visibility of public facilities through exterior windows, lobbies, and see-through fences, locating government services on major transportation corridors with round-the-clock public presence, and programs to increase community involvement with public spaces, such as tree plantings in parks by local groups and gardens for senior citizens.

Defensible space represented a radical departure from the fortress mentality that had obsessed planning authorities. Rather than hardening individual apartments, which isolated tenants from one another, defensible space encouraged social interaction and organization among tenants. Police were initially skeptical about Newman's recommendations. They felt that the solution to crime was more police patrols. Newman, on the other hand, felt that the only effective defense against crime was to strengthen the social organization among the tenants. The police would remain a secondary line of defense, but the first line of defense against crime would be the tenants themselves keeping watch over the project.

The theory allows for prediction regarding appropriate defensive measures in a variety of settings. The theory has some counter-intuitive aspects, as I learned in an incident on my campus.

LOCKING THE BATHROOM DOOR

A woman resident in one of the residence halls was assaulted in the shower. This created a wave of concern on the campus. Women's organizations demanded that the administration take action to improve the level of security for women in the residence halls. In response, the campus housing office decided to install locks on some of the bathroom doors. That way, if a student wanted to take a shower late at night or on weekends when few other people were around, the door could be locked from the inside to keep others out. This approach follows the familiar defensive strategy of hardening the target, that is, making vulnerable areas more secure.

While this sounded like a good security measure, defensible space principles recommend against it. According to defensible space theory, the locks might even make the bathrooms *less* secure by providing opportunities for a potential rapist to either hide inside the bathroom beforehand or force his way in behind an entering student to lock the door afterwards. On a nearby campus, there are round holes in several of the doors to the women's bathrooms where the locks were *removed* for security reasons. A woman was entering a bathroom in one of the buildings and a man came up from behind her, pushed her inside, locked the door, and assaulted her. Following this occurrence, authorities removed the locks from the bathroom doors. They felt that the best protection against sexual assault was the likelihood that other people could come upon the scene.

School officials in the United States are increasingly concerned about assaults and extortions occurring in bathrooms. Some fairly serious crimes were taking place in school restrooms that were hidden from the view of teachers and administrators. Some students were afraid to go to the restrooms for fear of being assaulted. The design strategy in Dade County, Florida was to remove obstacles to natural surveillance in order to decrease fear, increase use of space, and increase the risk to offenders of detection. Specific measures included removing entrance doors from restrooms, both to eliminate the perception of isolation created by the closed doors and to increase the risk of detection by eliminating the warning sound made when a door was opened. Existing portions of the anteroom wall were removed to increase natural surveillance. These changes did not interfere with the level of privacy required for restrooms. A right angle turn at the entrance provides visual privacy while increasing surveillance and the possibility of detecting serious criminal activity.[31]

I called the housing director on my campus to discuss the matter of the bathroom door locks with him. I argued that the installation of the locks might actually make the bathrooms *less* safe for the occupants. The housing director was surprised. He could not believe that I was seriously maintaining that interior locks would make a building *less* safe. Oscar Newman's ideas were also received with extreme skepticism by police when the ideas were first presented. The assumption that tenants could provide security when armed police had already failed to do so seemed ridiculous. The police solution was to bring in more officers on patrol. Unfortunately, this had been tried numerous times without improving the situation significantly.

I described Newman's theory to our student housing officials and cited several instances in which locks, partitions, and other interior barriers had been removed to increase occupants' security. Having a good theory with which to work allowed me to go beyond the superficial equation of locks with good security. The theory provided concepts, a body of research in relevant settings, and a vocabulary for making positive recommendations to the housing officials.

The result of my intervention was a compromise between defensible space principles and the politics of appearing to take some action in which one bathroom in each residence hall was provided with a lock that could be opened or closed by a key available to all residents.

BENEFITS TO THE BEHAVIORAL SCIENCES

While architecture was suffering from a crisis of purpose and was turning to the social sciences for assistance, social scientists had problems of their own. Although they had expanded tremendously in both number and influence during the postwar period, their work came under criticism from a number of sources. Those who wanted to solve pressing social and environmental problems were impatient with the researcher's air of detached objectivity. Questions were raised about the tendency of social scientists to locate the sources of problems in the personalities and backgrounds of those who suffered deprivation rather than in the institutions that shaped individuals and the society. Researchers published articles in journals read only by other researchers in which theoretical elegance and statistical analyses were emphasized at the cost of generalizability and utility. New models of training and investigation were needed that would connect in more tangible ways with the problems facing individuals and society.

At the same time, the ethics of behavioral research methods, as well as the value of the information yielded by the methods, came under scrutiny. The traditional approach had been to review previous studies, draw up an experimental plan, conduct a study, and publish the results. The information usually arrived too late to be of value to those caught in the problem or to those trying to solve it. The research results also came in a form unreadable and unusable by them. The emphasis in social science tended to be problem identification rather than solutions. Nevitt Sanford complained that his fellow psychologists "contributed to the dehumanization of our research subjects by reducing them to 'respondents' for the sake of enterprises that never yield any benefit to them."[1] Residents of crime-ridden neighborhoods, Native Americans on the reservation, impoverished rural people, alcoholics, and the aged felt that they were being studied to death without any positive changes in their lives. This contributed to a backlash that limited researcher access to many poor neighborhoods and institutional settings.

The social sciences responded to these criticisms in various ways. One approach was to become more interested in the physical conditions of people's lives. Environmental variables were absent from theories that described individuals and groups in the abstract rather than in concrete situations. As Roger Barker had pointed out, there was more consistency in the way in which two people behaved in a barber's chair than there was in the way that a single individual acted in the barber's chair and walking down the street.[2] Rudolf Moos, who began work as a clinical psychologist but later moved on to environmental psychology, said one of the major reasons for making the switch was that, "As a psychotherapist I found that I could neither understand nor predict the behavior of my patients in settings other than my office."[3] Within psychology, the new approach represented a departure from trait psychology, which stressed the importance of personality and social factors operating independently of situations. To fill this void where the physical environment was concerned, some social scientists turned to those professions whose expertise lay in planning and design. The motive on both sides of the relationship was the felt need to get one's own house in order rather than tangible gain. It was an altruistic association of individuals seeking assistance outside their own fields on problems within those fields.

When I first began working with architects, I had two objectives in mind. The first was to apply my own experiences and methods to a new field. I believed there were things that a psychologist could contribute to the design process, particularly in identifying user needs and determining how buildings worked from the standpoint of their occupants. The second objective was selfish from the standpoint of my own profession. I wanted to learn about physical design in order to enlarge the scope of my research and teaching. The social sciences had limited their usefulness by excluding information about the physical environment. With few exceptions, psychology theory ignored the physical grounding of human existence. Psychology seemed to be studying the psyche, now divided into parts called personality, learning, and perception, all of which were removed from anything tangible. An entire research literature of the laboratory was written without regard to behavior in the world outside, creating an unbridgeable gulf between the study of learning (nonsense syllables in darkened rooms) and what teachers did in the classroom, between the study of abnormal behavior (how schizophrenics responded to exotic test questions) and what psychotherapists did in their offices, and between the study of perception (simple designs presented in a fixed viewer to a seated individual) and how people in motion experienced streets, neighborhoods, and cities. Enlargement of scale and research on natural environments were two of the major contributions of environmental psychology to social science.

Harold Proshansky, one of the pioneers in environmental psychology, became convinced that laboratory simulation produced little, if any, accumulative scientific knowledge about the behavior of individuals or groups. The price for "scientific respectability was too high," Proshansky concluded. "In the process of adapting issues for laboratory study, an unreal world was studied."[4] Psychological journals were described as "full of research that is methodologically impeccable and intellectually vapid."[5] The distinguishing characteristics of the behavioral scientists who became involved in the social design movement was that they were cross-disciplinary in outlook, more interested in real-world problems than in the laboratory, and committed to solving problems. All of this was a departure from the dominant outlook in the behavioral sciences at the time, which was disciplinary, laboratory oriented, and more concerned with problem identification than with solutions. Environmental research was not considered a threat by traditionalists in the behavioral sciences, who were accustomed to some of their flock straying from conventional ground. Often it seemed that the productive theories and methods could be found at the intersection between the familiar and the new. As older fields and conceptions reach out to touch new problems, they are changed and broadened.

Clinical psychologists have become more aware of the importance of neighborhood and social support systems in maintaining mental health. Some of them looked critically at the design and layout of their own offices to determine how clients were affected by the spatial arrangement, color, texture, and visual aesthetics.[6] Twenty years ago it was common to find therapists treating their clients in drab institutional rooms. Under the supposition that the only thing that mattered was the interaction between the therapist and the client, such barren quarters could be justified. However, with a new view that included people-place relationships, the treatment milieu became a focus of attention. Sociological theories of interaction and relationship have also been enriched by the inclusion of tangible elements of the urban environment, including house location, parks and plazas, and physical barriers. The scope of geography has been widened by studies of people's mental images of their surroundings. These new concerns complemented traditional ways of looking at problems.

Researchers currently are doing work on problems as varied as airport noise, rush hour commuting, crime prevention in public housing, and crowding in the national parks. It has been useful to get some psychologists out of the laboratory into the real world. Besides providing fresh air and exercise, it has provided exposure to situations not found in the laboratory. It has also fostered the development of methods for studying natural behavior in a nonintrusive manner. There are still not enough data to write a definitive psychology of natural behavior, but the time is coming when it will be feasible.

Much of the task of translating the new findings back into the parent disciplines remains to be done. There are some fascinating applications of wilderness research in anthropology and psychology. Some of the reasons that people hike into remote areas are to have contact with nature untamed, to simplify lives and relationships, and to test inner strength. The strong, positive attitudes that growing plants elicit is virtually unexplored territory for the behavioral sciences, except for some ethnobotanists, who have largely confined their efforts to food-producing plants. It is clearly not only the visual properties of plants that make them so attractive, since artificial grass and plastic trees tend to be disliked, but rather, that greenery seems to tap into life and growth. Historic preservation is another issue that reaches deep into the human psyche. What is so appealing about a building that is connected to earlier events? What does it mean to walk down hallways trod on by the great artists, writers, scientists, or political leaders of another generation? What does it mean to live in such a building? What is the difference between visiting an older building in decrepit condition, left to age without human intervention; an older building restored to its original state and used as a museum; and a Disneyland replica of an older structure? The differences between the experiences in each type of building will tell us something about people's attitudes towards history and culture.

There is increasing discussion of environmental influences in social science courses. For many years I've taught Abnormal Psychology from an environmental perspective, which I believe has enriched the course. Much of what is termed disturbed behavior is a response to external pressures. It is hard to be healthy and happy living in a cesspool. When people are surrounded by ugliness, brutality, and meanness, they are not likely to emerge as loving, caring individuals. Although heroes can triumph in spite of poor conditions, we should not design a world solely for heroes; most heroes survive not because of adversity, but in spite of it.

PROFESSIONAL IDENTITY

Professionals employed in interdisciplinary settings need to know who they are professionally. When clinical psychologists began working in mental hospitals in large numbers there were many problems of role and identity. The fact that they wore white coats and were called "doctors" created confusion between them and psychiatrists. Those clinical psychologists who became mini-psychiatrists contributed little to their own profession, since they tended to employ models borrowed from another field (medicine). Fortunately there were other clinical psychologists who did not garb themselves in the cloak of psychiatry and found ways to make contributions within their own discipline. Instead of using medical treatments, they developed behavioral methods for handling problems. Some became milieu therapists, whose goal was to create therapeutic environments. Others developed behavioral treatments such as token economies and reinforcement schedules for reducing disturbed behavior. Many concentrated on psychological testing and research aimed at understanding the causes and effects of mental disorders.

The same pitfalls existed in social design for psychologists who were employed in architecture schools and architects and planners who had worked on behavioral problems. The goal in social design was not homogenization of separate professions, but an enlarged vision in each through a cross-disciplinary perspective and new approaches and concepts. The landscape architect who became interested in people in parks was still a landscape architect and needed sound technical knowledge in site design, plant material, grading, drainage, and the like, as well as the ability to work with neighborhood associations. The psychologist teaching in an architecture department still had to be knowledgeable in the concepts, methods, and findings of academic psychology in order to apply them to new problems.

Various models were proposed for incorporating social design into curricula and practice. Social design could be viewed as a specialty area within architecture or psychology, as a new profession, or as a broadened outlook. Each view had different implications for training. When the social design movement first took shape, many of its adherents saw the possibility of a new profession midway between design and behavioral science. There was no consensus on its name, whether it should be called social ecology, person-environment relations, or behavioral architecture, but there was the hope that it would lead to new careers for graduates of the new interdisciplinary programs. Designers and behavioral scientists were attracted to these programs for somewhat different reasons, but in each field it was a means of remedying deficiencies in existing training institutions. Design curricula were very strong in application and weak in theory and research. Even today the terms "research architect" and "design theorist" lack clear meaning. Academic programs in the behavioral sciences were heavily geared to theory and research and weak in application. Those attracted to social design from architecture and planning were primarily interested in its academic content, while those who came from the behavioral sciences were interested in application.[7]

Consulting with architects made me aware of the different problem-solving styles in our respective professions. Many of us in the social sciences had become spatial illiterates. We could not express ourselves visually or graphically. We had developed abstract and critical faculties at the expense of our imagery. This was most evident in our teaching. A blind student could get as much from a psychology lecture as a sighted student. Social science journals are largely devoid of photographs but are replete with tables and numbers. Most of the slides that I have seen at social science meetings have depicted columns of numbers. This does not seem to be the optimal use of visual presentation.

Professor Roger Bailey, who started the first architectural psychology program in the nation at the University of Utah, felt that it was essential for psychologists, if they wanted to work with architects, to learn how architects think and to learn about the design process. Bailey put it this way:

> *I would have the psychologists understand the language of architects. I would have them take our orientation course in the School of Architecture which is aimed at developing a language that we all understand. The meaning of the words we use can be quite complex sometimes. Next I would have them take the first design course which is really an exercise in just logical thinking on paper, with a pencil. They need those tools if they are going to understand the people they are trying to work with, to know how they think.*[8]

My own teaching in psychology has been enriched by association with designers. I show slides and drawings more often then I had before. These are, incidentally, pictures of real scenes and people rather than columns of numbers. I do not demean verbal or quantitative expression. At heart I am a writer and researcher who has come, through association with designers, to appreciate how visual material can enhance learning.

The enrichment that resulted from the association between designers and social scientists has proceeded in both directions. If the information exchange has seemed lopsided, it is only because social scientists are more verbal and have tended to dominate the print media. There are quite a few designers who have been strongly influenced by social science and have made efforts to integrate it into their professional practice and design teaching, for instance, George Agron, Chris Arnold, David Chapin, Don Conway, Gerald Davis, Michael Durkin, Randy Hester, Herbert McLaughlin, Robin Moore, Louis Sauer, Murray Silverstein, Patrick Sullivan, Sim van der Ryn, and so on. There are also social scientists who have gained some understanding about the nature of the design process, for example, Kathryn Anthony, Bob Bechtel, Frank Becker, David Canter, Yvonne Clearwater, Alton De Long, Rachel Kaplan, Gary Winkel, John Zeisel, and others. These are behavioral scientists who have learned to some degree how to "think like architects" without losing their behavioral science skills. They can credit their increased appreciation of the importance of the physical conditions of people's lives, the understanding of how color, lighting, and texture can affect mood and behavior, and recognition that visual thinking can be useful in problem-solving in their association with designers. David Canter believes that "as more and more psychologists are being called upon either in a consultative capacity or as teachers to students of engineering, architecture, or planning, it is likely that the demands made on each of them in this context will cause them to reconsider much of what they accept as valuable and to re-examine the subject matter of their profession in an attempt to orient it more towards real-world decision-making."[9]

QUESTIONS THAT WILL NOT GO AWAY

Whenever user consultation in design decisions is proposed, someone is likely to ask whether or not this will increase productivity. It is not enough that people appreciate being involved in decisions that will affect their lives and will be more satisfied with the outcome when they do; the questioner wants to know whether this is profitable in some measurable way. If we design hospitals that take into account patient needs, will this improve recovery rates or shorten the duration of treatment? If a school has attractive and stimulating classrooms, will this increase student test scores? If we allow residents to participate in neighborhood planning, will this improve their mental, physical, or economic health? I've even been asked if there was proof that French Provincial decor would improve productivity. An interior design firm specializing in French Provincial believed that this would create a more homey office situation and thereby improve performance.

I have been wrestling with questions like these for more than twenty years. The issue is whether giving people what they want in the way of environmental amenities will improve their productivity. The query recurs so frequently that it must be answered. There is no way that someone involved in social design can avoid it. Curiously it is not often asked of the formalistic designer. The trendy architect who proposes an unusual shape or decorative style is not going to be asked whether this will reduce worker absenteeism or improve the job performance of the occupants. Questions about the people inside seem irrelevant or impertinent to one who designs for a jury of other architects. The chief concern of the client in such cases is how the unusual appearance will affect the corporate image. Although those who take a fine arts approach to architecture can attempt to ignore occupant response in discussions of their work, this is not true of a social designer whose justification is occupant satisfaction. This results in a double standard, in which the work of the social designer is evaluated in terms of its success in meeting occupant needs, while buildings by formalistic designers are judged on the basis of appearance according to aesthetic criteria.

Before trying to answer the productivity question, one must first recognize the crucial difference between user response to a building and productivity gains. The behavioral sciences have developed various methods for assessing response to the environment.

These methods include interviews, questionnaires, rating scales, behavioral maps, interaction counts, and the like. However, the productivity question does not concern user response in general, but specifically the measurable gains in output. The questioner does not want to know whether patients and staff are more satisfied in their new hospital building or whether office workers dress up more in their new quarters, but rather whether patients get well faster and the office workers will achieve more in their new offices. It is objective gains in output and not experience that is at issue.

The productivity question assumes some type of activity on the part of employees, the value of which can be measured and traced to specific design elements. These assumptions are questionable in many instances. When there is no specific product involved, as in an office building or civic center, it will be difficult to measure performance. Even when there is a product, there is the problem of relating increases or decreases in output to environmental factors. When people move into a new building or neighborhood, there are many changes taking place at once and it will be difficult to identify those responsible for their actions. The physical environment is only one of many things that affects performance and it does this mostly from beyond the focus of awareness. Architecture, as Ada Louise Huxtable reminds us, is the art we take for granted.[1] It does not have much observable impact on performance by itself, at least within ordinary ranges of stimulation. Ceilings that are four feet in height will hinder employee effectiveness, but it will be difficult to prove that there is any difference in employee output between ceilings that are seven feet and seven-and-a-half feet tall. Correspondingly, walls in an office that are scarlet or jet black will probably increase lateness, absenteeism, and turnover, but it will be difficult to demonstrate performance differences between pastel blue, pastel yellow, or salmon walls. There will be differences in consumer acceptance of these options, but the basis of the productivity question is not consumer acceptance but tangible gains in output.

Another problem with the productivity question involves the nature of proof that design makes a difference. Generally the standards of science require that all the important factors can be controlled and that the researcher must undertake numerous replications and variations of the same experiment to be certain of the results. It is not likely that architectural research can meet these standards. The cost of large physical systems makes it difficult to apply the ideal laboratory model for experimentation. Even in the case of single design elements, such as color or illumination, the range of variation is so vast as to be unmanageable. There not only are myriad blue or green hues, but each will be perceived differently depending upon the illumination, texture, noise level, and so on. The laboratory model is appropriate for variables that can be stripped to their bare essentials and manipulated singly or in combination, but it is not useful for measuring performance gains on the scale of a building or neighborhood.[2]

Sometimes the problem in answering the productivity question is not that information on productivity gains is unavailable, but that the search is not cost effective. With unlimited time and resources, I believe that it could be proven that allowing employees to have a voice in selecting furnishings and arranging work stations would reduce turnover and absenteeism. This would require the active cooperation of management in perhaps 40 offices in various parts of the country, including the authority to designate which employees would be given choices and which would not. The experiment would last ten years and would cost, if the actual furnishings themselves were included, tens of millions of dollars. The research aspects of the project alone would require a budget of several million dollars. If the gods were smiling, the results might show an average turnover or absenteeism difference of perhaps 2 to 3 percent between offices that were allowed to participate and those that were not allowed. This is my guesstimate of the portion of job satisfaction related to absenteeism or turnover that is attributable to employees' satisfaction with furnishings. If differences were found, critics might charge that they were "Hawthorne Effects." This criticism will be discussed in further detail in Chapter 6, and refers to the possibility that such changes are due to management's interest in the workers' welfare rather than to the physical changes. Attempting to meet this objection might require removal of the new furnishings at some later point in the experiment. All this would make interpretation of the results very difficult. I seriously doubt that the information from such a massive and arbitrary intervention in people's lives (and a true experiment would have to be arbitrary in designating which offices were to be changed), could be justified ethically or financially. The study could be done but that does not mean that it should be done.

Following are various answers that can be given to the productivity question.

A. The case has already been proven. For me as a researcher, this is a dangerous and irresponsible answer, since it cannot be backed up with sufficient hard evidence. There are some studies showing performance gains through good design. One researcher found that brightening up a classroom improved student test scores, but other researchers do not find this.[3] Efforts by courts to relieve overcrowding in prisons and jails has brought down tension levels and reduced assaults.[4] The renovation of a hospital ward, which included random assignment of patients to the improved ward and to the old ward, found more social activities, more patient-staff interaction, higher morale, and more personalization of living areas on the remodeled ward than on its drab counterpart, and the renovation of a building lobby dramatically increased its use.[5] The evidence on productivity gains may be suggestive but it is not conclusive.

B. More research is needed. Twenty years ago, if the productivity issue was raised, it was possible to cite the need for further research. This was an optimistic era when science seemed to promise answers for all questions. If environmental researchers were given sufficient time and resources, they would be able to demonstrate that good design improved performance. Much of the early research on environmental influences had been sponsored by the National Institutes of Health. The hope existed that it would be possible to demonstrate that well-designed hospitals would speed recovery. As I became aware of the difficulties of doing systematic studies that would yield conclusive results on the scale of buildings, I tried to point this out to the questioner. There were so many factors that influenced a patient's length of stay, including the enormous daily cost and the availability of insurance coverage, that it would be unrealistic to expect a pleasant room or the presence or absence of reading lights to have a measurable impact on the duration of a patient's treatment. It would be possible to measure *proximate effects,* such as the amount of time spent reading as a function of the availability of bed lamps, but this skirted the productivity issue. The questioner was not interested in whether bed lamps encouraged reading, which might be readily conceded, but whether this speeded up recovery.

I strongly endorse the idea of further research into the connection between places and behavior. This important and useful line of inquiry should be continued and expanded. It will eventually provide findings that enrich theory and practice in design and the behavioral sciences, but I am not sure that it will yield conclusive proof of productivity gains in many situations. There are too many extraneous and uncontrollable factors and too wide a gulf between design and performance for this relationship to be proven beyond doubt.

C. User input does not cost additional money. In many projects a great deal of money is invested in the planning stage without ever obtaining systematic surveys of user needs or wants. Further research is needed on the economics of user participation as compared with other methods of planning, which tend to treat it in a haphazard manner or not at all. Kathryn Anthony documented how behavioral consultation reduced overall cost on several projects by eliminating unnecessary features.[6] Attractive buildings that are appreciated by their occupants need not cost any more than ugly or dysfunctional buildings and may sometimes cost less. As far as interiors go, bright colors cost the same as dull colors, and imaginative layouts are often no more expensive than those that are boring and institutional. Many projects follow the old army expression, "It doesn't have to be cheap, it just has to look cheap." If user consultation is not going to cost more money than other planning methods, and the final product is not more expensive because of it, then the productivity question can be put aside.

D. User participation requires no further justification. People in a democratic society should be consulted about changes that affect their lives. To design a school building and not consult teachers and students, or to design a hospital without consulting patients and staff seems morally and ethically untenable. One should not have to defend such consultation and participation on the grounds of increased output.

E. Don't ask me, ask the occupants. Another way of handling the productivity question is to find someone with a direct stake in the outcome to answer it. Instead of asking a researcher to prove that participation in design decisions will make patients healthier or workers more productive, the designer should seek input from potential occupants who have a vested interest in their own comfort and well-being. Let the employer try to justify a dark building or lack of soundproofing to the employees who will spend 40 hours a week inside rather than asking a researcher for evidence that improvements will raise profits. Because the employees will have less interest than management in graphs showing increased production, an effective strategy for those who advocate user input is to develop a constituency among the users for increasing their role in the design process.

F. Productivity is not the issue. When I discussed the productivity question with an anthropologist who had spent time among native peoples in northern Canada, he nodded sympathetically and attributed my problem to the white man's obsession with quantification. For the natives with whom he had lived, it was sufficient that things worked. White people had to prove this in terms of numbers.

Assuming that it was a good year for hunting, the anthropologist immediately wanted to know how many shots were fired, how many birds were killed, how many of these would be eaten on the spot, and how many would be prepared for the long winter ahead. The natives could not understand why anyone needed this information. It seemed odd that a grown man would spend his time asking trivial questions rather than being out gathering food and doing survival chores.

Part of me responds to the productivity question as the native people reacted to the anthropologist. Some things cannot be proven in terms of numbers, at least not to the point at which the results justify the effort that went into collecting the information. Perhaps we should stop looking for gains in productivity and concentrate on identifying those qualities that make places satisfying, exciting, and aesthetically appealing to their occupants without worrying whether this will improve mental health, reduce juvenile delinquency, or raise the gross national product. John Ruskin had asked his fellow architects, "What should we call ourselves? Men? I think not. The right name for us would be—numerators and denominators. Vulgar fractions."[7] Those who ask the productivity question would like to put dollar signs on positive experiences. Sometimes this may be possible, but more often it is not. I admire those rugged realists who try to find selfish reasons why people should behave altruistically, who argue that preserving historical buildings is good for business, and that saving other species is really a way of saving ourselves, yet I regard this reasoning as a trap. Arguing strictly from the standpoint of self-interest, it is probably easier to make a case for removing a historical building than for extensive rehabilitation, and the dollar value of most exotic species is minimal. Usually it makes more sense to justify good causes on the basis of valid good reasons than for invalid selfish reasons.

G. Leap of faith. Rather than looking for output gains that can be attributed to specific architectural elements, we should concentrate our efforts on experiences and behavior and assume that they have some relationship to performance even if we cannot measure it and establish causality. Through some combination of laboratory simulations and field tests, we can identify those colors, textures, lines, and proportions that people prefer. There is a need for good case studies of successful places that can enrich the image banks of designers and that can be shown to clients. Research can be used to identify airport departure lounges that can allay the fears of anxious individuals and the types of apartments associated with higher levels of tenant satisfaction. A leap of faith is necessary to go beyond the improved attitude and morale of the occupants to their output. My experience has been that this is not a problem for many clients for whom it is enough to know that their employees, customers, or tenants are happy with a building. The San Francisco headquarters of the Bank of America abandoned open offices for attorneys because they could not attract the brightest students from Stanford and Boalt Hall law schools, who refused to work in open offices. At Mobil Oil headquarters in Houston, where there was an almost 30 percent turnover among geologists, exit interviews revealed that dissatisfaction with open offices was frequently cited as a reason for leaving.[8] That these problems in recruitment and retention stemmed directly from environmental factors is difficult to prove according to the canons of experimental science, but fortunately many corporate clients do not require this standard of proof. They are willing to make a leap of faith from reasonable statements about motives or morale to the indicated causes.

The linguistic root of *truth* is belief or trust, while *proof* comes from a Middle English word meaning trial or test. Science is concerned with testing relationships according to certain rules of evidence. The question for the scientist is not whether something is true but whether it has been proven according to specified criteria. When it comes to art or architecture, other methods may be superior to experimentation for reaching truth. John Eberhard advocates a new type of science that supplements quantitative information with poetic and artistic insights, and gives credibility to human experiences of environment.[9] "An architectural idea," declared Edward Larrabee Barnes, "has something to do with scale, movement, light, procession. It is something that cannot be expressed in painting, or in sculpture, or in music."[10] Barnes might have added that it may not be expressible through science either. Reason provides the ground from which the vault is made from the general to the particular, the abstract to the tangible, the past to the future. Intuition, dreams, and hopes provide the stamina and the inspiration for making the leap. Rudolf Arnheim has his own solution to the issue of proof in architecture:

> *The qualities that carry values can be described with considerable precision. But many of these descriptions cannot be quantitatively confirmed by the measuring or counting of data. They share this trait with many other facts of mind and nature, and it does not prevent them from existing or being important. Nor does a lack of numerical proof exclude them from objective discussion. The "ostensive" method of arguing with the index finger by pointing to perceivable facts, making comparisons, and drawing attention to relevant relations is a legitimate way of furthering understanding by common effort.*[11]

HORSE-AND-CART

Another important issue in urban planning and architecture is the priority to be assigned to physical changes. How much money should be invested in buildings when there are so many urgent social problems still unsolved? What programs must be cut in order to preserve a historic house or purchase sculpture for a civic building or shield freeway residents against unwanted noise? Would it not be preferable to put the limited amount of money available directly into service programs rather than into structures? People can survive noxious environments; great artists have painted masterpieces in unheated garrets; and Albert Schweitzer won a Nobel Prize for healing natives in a crudely built hospital in Africa. It is possible to argue that a certain degree of privation will encourage creativity. The critic declares that spending money on buildings, parks, or street furniture is putting the cart before the horse. "Brains, not bricks," was the way Karl Menninger expressed this view.

Buildings are expensive, and some specialized buildings are very expensive. A new jail may cost $80,000 per cell, and someone is going to ask whether it would not be more effective to develop community service and restitution programs. When an addition to an existing hospital is proposed, someone will advocate directing the money into preventive health and community nutrition. When the pot of money available for education is shrinking, how can the value of preventive maintenance of the physical plant be compared with the preservation of academic programs? The earlier discussion of productivity is relevant to the horse-and-cart problem. If it could be demonstrated that student performance declines in poorly designed classrooms or that employees will quit if their working stations are badly laid out, then we could assign good design a high priority. Unfortunately, as we have seen, the connection between environmental design and performance is not so simple. Occupants can tolerate a good deal of discomfort before they lower their performance. In most settings, architecture ranks below other factors in importance for human health and well-being. Of course if the heating system is not operating or if the roof leaks, these are likely to be serious matters for the occupants and the owner; but in the typical building, where all the systems are operating to some degree, the physical aspects and especially the aesthetics are likely to be taken for granted. The decor of an airline terminal building will be less of an influence on passenger satisfaction than ticket price, aircraft safety, and the punctuality of the airline. Most passengers would prefer an on-time airline with a good safety record located in a dinky terminal to one with unsafe and tardy service with a large attractive departure lounge. Fortunately there is no need to make such choices. It should be possible to have efficiency, safety, and good aesthetics without trading off one against another.

In responding to the horse-and-cart issue I do not visualize a single road to Utopia containing one horse and one cart advancing directly ahead. Rather, I see many roads and many horses pulling many carts in many directions. Some horses will necessarily be in front of some carts and others behind, and some will be moving more slowly than others. The different approaches to improving society need not be mutually exclusive. One can upgrade teacher training and also design more functional school buildings. One can give factory workers more control over the production line as well as reduce pollution in the workplace. Such measures are interdependent. Giving workers a voice in environmental decision-making is likely to increase their awareness of the value of input into other areas, such as streamlining production and technical innovation.

I do not believe that all those who are interested in social change should devote their attention to buildings. This is one approach among many others to the improvement of society. It is more suitable for those in architecture and planning than for most other people. Fortunately it is not a restrictive approach. Unless a designer wears blinders, larger social issues inevitably arise in the course of a specific project. No one can be involved in the design of a convalescent home without considering the plight of the elderly, or in planning a low-income housing project without facing up to the issue of segregation of the poor in undesirable neighborhoods.

Improving any single factor in a larger system may not amount to much on a percentage basis, but it is still worthwhile and necessary for those concerned with that specific aspect. I prefer attractive to ugly post offices, but I don't believe that attractive buildings are an important issue for most postal users. Yet it is legitimate, proper, and necessary for someone in the postal service to be concerned with building design. If the architecture of a post office contributes only 5 percent to the overall satisfaction level of customers, it is still important for the designer and the postal manager to be concerned with that 5 percent. Such changes also tend to be synergistic. Improvement in one aspect of a person's life is likely to be associated with improvement in other aspects. An attractive post office is likely to make people conscious of the need to upgrade other public facilities.

If improved customer satisfaction through good design can be documented in one post office, the lessons can be applied elsewhere. I can justify my role in improving something 5 percent so long as I can combine the percentages from different projects. The generality of findings among building types allows a greater investment of time and effort in a particular project than would be warranted by the number of occupants in a specific building.

CONCLUSION

Following the distinction between questions of fact and value, the productivity question deals with fact (Is there a measurable link between user input and improved performance?), and the horse-and-cart question deals with the value of investing money in environments that satisfy occupant needs.

While I am pessimistic about the long-range possibilities for demonstrating productivity effects of design changes according to accepted standards of scientific proof, I am optimistic regarding the possibilities for demonstrating behavioral effects of design changes. We can show, for example, that a new color scheme and clear orientation aids improve morale among nurses, physicians, and hospital patients, and that students will be more satisfied and participate more fully in an attractive "soft" classroom compared with the typical institutional straight-row classroom prevalent in most schools. My experience has been that most policy makers will be satisfied with such proximate measures of design success. Researchers who want to document the behavioral effects of design changes should choose proximate indicators close to what policy makers care about, that is, with good "face validity."

Productivity and the horse-and-cart are two of many unanswered questions that must be addressed if social design is to mature. Other questions include the optimal size of neighborhoods and cities, the proper balance of built and natural features in the landscape, and the role of buildings as cultural and historical artifacts. These questions are more fundamental and general than those that most researchers are addressing. None of them will have a clear conclusive answer. Designers must still take them seriously if only because other people will ask them. To ignore these questions without understanding their implications will be perceived as arrogance.

USER NEEDS ANALYSIS (UNA)

Behavioral scientists were first brought into the design process to shed light on the needs of future occupants. Since psychologists had expert knowledge on the ways in which people responded to light, color, and proportion, sociologists about the nature of social organization in neighborhoods, and anthropologists on buildings as symbols and artifacts, it was hoped that they would be able to apply this knowledge to the design process. This approach faltered for a number of reasons. The findings collected in basic research could not be applied with any confidence. Color perception was one of the oldest topics in experimental psychology, but if an experimental psychologist were asked to specify the colors that should be used in a bus station, the answer was likely to be vague and uncertain. Nor was research on space perception, another traditional research topic, useful for understanding orientation in buildings and neighborhoods. Sociologists had done considerable research on neighborhood networks, but their findings were usually too general to assist the city planner.

The information in basic research studies was presented in a form and style that was almost incomprehensible to anyone except advanced students in the individual disciplines. This is not a special failing of the behavioral sciences, for it is true of most fields of scholarship in which specialists write exclusively for other specialists. Some translation is necessary in order to make existing information useful to practitioners. In making this translation, researchers became aware of the limitations not only of existing data, but of the methods available for answering the questions asked.

Needs analysis went through several stages in its evolution and is still changing. At the outset, designers relied on needs they inferred or extrapolated from basic research studies and from theory. More recent approaches have tended to dwell less upon inferred needs and more upon direct expression of people's wants, which are obtained through surveys or by the involvement of users in the design process. The relationship between needs and wants is full of pitfalls for the unwary. A need is something basic, fundamental, and enduring, as in the need for shelter, sustenance, and social contact, while a want is an expressed preference, and thus is likely to be specific, transient, and more easily changed, as in the desire for a particular brand of food or clothing style. Human needs have traditionally been regarded as more acceptable topics of study than wants in the behavioral sciences. The investigation of preferences is considered to be a second-rate applied task, more akin to marketing than to serious scholarship. This dual standard has its roots in the platonic view that appearances are deceptive and ephemeral and that the important reality lies underneath. However in some specific cases a firm distinction between needs and wants is difficult to maintain.

Some architects and urban planners looked to the behavioral sciences not for specific bits of information that could be applied on particular projects but for general theories of human behavior that could be generalized to many settings. Some designers found what they wanted to know about perception in the writings of James J. Gibson and Rudolf Arnheim; about the desire for stimulation and variety in the work of D. O. Hebb and Daniel Berlyne; and about social life within neighborhoods from Herbert Gans and Louis Wirth. This interest in general theories remains strong today and co-exists with the desire for place-specific information.

A mutual learning regarding what each can obtain from the other has occurred in the dialogue between designers and behavioral scientists. Initially, architects complained that the social scientists' answers were too general, tentative, and often came too late to be useful. Behavioral scientists criticized the architects' queries as being too specific, time-pressured, and deterministic in assuming a direct connection between building elements and behavioral patterns. One of the most useful contributions that social scientists have made to design was to point out that design does not alone determine behavior. Even when it strongly influences how people behave, the effects are not direct but are mediated through psychosocial factors; for example, different people will be affected differently by the same building, depending upon whether they are alone or in a group, happy or sad, or are visiting for the first time or are accustomed to the place. Eventually those designers who wanted to collaborate with behavioral scientists learned how to ask questions that could be answered within the time frame, methods, and data base of the social sciences, and those behavioral scientists active in the collaboration learned to produce timely and relevant reports. All this took time and patience on everyone's part. Effective collaboration between people in different fields, especially those as distinct in training and temperament as design and behavioral science, does not come easily.

NEEDS ASSESSMENT SURVEY

Another approach to needs analysis came not from basic research or from theory, but from marketing, and involved asking people what they wanted in the way of work or living space. This blurs the distinction between needs and wants, since it assumes that people's responses will bear some relationship to both. Studies of expressed preference are of interest to the social scientist and useful to industry. The value of such studies increases if they identify the particular properties inherent in the object on which the preference or rejection is based.[1] Technically it would have been more accurate to title this chapter *Wants Analysis,* but I have followed the conventional practice of discussing "needs," since, from a practical standpoint, needs are more saleable than wants. Managers are more likely to respond positively when they are told that employees need something than when they are told that employees want it. The latter statement is likely to provoke the response, "Yes, we know they want it, but we can't afford to give it to them. However, if our workers need it then that is another matter." In some ways this is a semantics game, more akin to diplomacy than science. If the client probes beneath the question and asks whether the employees *really need* the item, the speaker must have cogent answers ready or be prepared to retreat.

Within industries that sell to the consumer, needs analysis is an essential part of product development. Large corporations undertake consumer surveys through a marketing department to identify existing and unmet demands. An entire methodology has been developed around measures of consumer acceptance in the marketplace. The approach combines the initial demand analysis with market testing of different models on a trial basis. The large costs of architectural systems probably means that the building itself will be the test. However an early needs analysis to ascertain what consumers want is still feasible.

Economists speak of actual behavior in the marketplace as "revealed preferences," meaning that the behavior of people in purchasing goods and services reveals their wants and preferences.[2] This approach is not valid in most designed spaces that are not "purchased" by their occupants. Nor can people's attitudes towards the architecture or interior layout be discerned by how long they remain inside. The failure of market mechanisms to reveal preferences and levels of occupant satisfaction with designed spaces created a niche for formal techniques for gauging occupant response. Most designers claim to be meeting market demands to some degree, but the distinctive feature of UNA (user needs analysis) is that it is carried out in a systematic manner. This requires the use of standardized techniques for collecting information (interviews, questionnaires, and so on) and some sampling of occupants and their activities. Without formal procedures for selecting people to be interviewed and ways of asking questions, the technique does not qualify as a UNA.

Becker distinguishes between *user input,* which refers to comments from those who will actually occupy a planned or renovated facility when it is completed, and *consumer input,* which is given by those who are similar, along explicit dimensions, to potential occupants, but who will not themselves occupy the planned facility.[3] It is not always safe to assume that input from potential occupants of a setting will be more relevant to the design process than input from those in similar facilities. It may be that the potential occupants have never experienced a building of the same type before. For example, asking teachers and students in a traditional school building what their space and environmental needs would be in an open-plan school building with modular pods housing three grades each may turn up little useful information, *unless* potential occupants are given some education or experience with open-plan school buildings. Consulting with potential occupants is *always* desirable when it is possible, both because of the possibility of securing useful information about the residents and their space needs, and because it will satisfy people's desire to be consulted about changes that affect their lives.

An assumption in a needs assessment survey is that potential occupants know what they want and can communicate this to an interviewer. In cases where people are turned off to their physical surroundings and alienated from the decision-making process, this assumption is not valid. Most people asked about civic improvements will respond hesitantly and tentatively. They have not given much thought to these matters. There was no reason for them to be concerned since their opinions had not mattered. Even if they have an idea about what they want, they may not have the concepts to convey this to a designer. This calls for some patience on the part of the interviewer in asking the right questions and in waiting for answers to come, just as listening to the speaker of another language requires special patience.

Drawings and models can make design alternatives more tangible to the prospective occupants. People can be shown various options and asked to choose among them. The occupant can move around parts of a scale model or even take part in a slide simulation study showing how a building façade will appear in different exterior colors. Rather than asking people what colors they desire, which will produce stereotyped responses confined largely to primary colors, it is more effective to show people a color palette and ask them to select specific combinations. Such procedures are more time-consuming and costly than questionnaires, but they stimulate greater involvement and interest.

The needs survey will be more meaningful when the designer has spent some time among the occupants and knows how they think and express themselves. It would be extremely difficult to conduct a needs analysis in a specialized building without knowing the technical vocabulary of the residents. Experiencing how people use space as a preliminary to design is exemplified in the work of landscape architect Lawrence Halprin.[4] Before the drawings are put on paper, Halprin and his staff go out into settings like those for which a design is to be conceived and spend time there in order to develop a choreography of people-place relationships in which movement patterns are paramount. Halprin has used these *choreographs* to design such successful places as San Francisco's Ghiradelli Square and the Forecourt and Lovejoy Fountains in Portland, Oregon. These works illustrate that a design that takes people's activities and interests into account can be exciting, attractive, and in the case of commercial buildings, economically successful. What Halprin did *not* do was create sculptural forms in his studio and impose them on a location.

It has been argued that architects should live in the types of buildings that they are designing. The Urban Development Corporation in New York City has required this of their architects for public housing projects for some time. This is not a formal needs analysis, but it is one way of ensuring that the architect comes into direct contact with future occupants. Living among the occupants works better in some places than in others. In preparing an architectural plan for a university, architect Neal Deasy lived for a week in a dormitory and took all his meals in the dining hall.[5] Dressed in a conservative tweed suit and vest, he felt he was "as conspicuous as a piebald aardvark." The approach proved more successful in the outdoor areas of the campus. Deasy started his observations at 7:30 a.m. and concluded at 10 p.m. He followed a set course through the campus and noted what was taking place, who was involved, and what they were doing. Photographs were taken at key locations and were printed on inexpensive proof sheets. Having the photographs independently analyzed served as a check on the observer. The pictures were useful in transmitting the architect's recommendations to his client. Photographs are often more persuasive than words for conveying the realities of human behavior, especially when the behavior is at odds with conventional expectations about how an area is being used.

Kathryn Anthony has been documenting the costs and benefits of needs analysis in several construction projects undertaken by the architectural office of Patrick Sullivan Associates in San Luis Obispo, California.[6] She has been able to show how the needs analysis lowered project costs. In the case of two jails, the research showed that a lower level of security hardware and construction were feasible, and in the construction of a city hall, how similar types of work stations could be consolidated. Anthony also presents some interesting statistics on the hours required for behavioral consultation. The Kings County Juvenile Center was constructed in 1981, with behavioral consultation costing $90 a square foot instead of the projected $125 a square foot. The client was billed for 472 hours of consultation (principal researcher, 141 hours, project manager, 214 hours, research assistant, 37 hours, administration and clerical assistance, 80 hours). On the city hall project, which was scaled down 15 percent because of the efficiency of the open-office modular work stations recommended by the researchers, the client was billed for under 1,300 consultant hours.

A criticism of needs analysis is that it will awaken false hopes if people assume that they will always get what they request. This expectation can be avoided, or at least minimized, by a clear statement in the survey that it may not be possible to fulfill everyone's wishes and by clearly stating at the outset the scope, resources, and limitations of the proposed project. On the other hand, it is necessary that people believe that their suggestions will receive a fair hearing. Otherwise their replies are not likely to be very useful for the UNA. I was part of a team that conducted a survey among a group of long-term employees in a company with very paternalistic attitudes. Even though we assured people that they were going to receive most of what they asked for, many workers doubted that we could deliver on our promise. They had worked for the company for so long that they knew that this didn't happen. Residents of low-income neighborhoods have been surveyed so often without tangible improvement in their situation that they will have little confidence that another survey is going to make a difference. Such cynicism can be overcome only if the survey team itself believes that the results are important and useful.

A questionnaire is not a ballot and a survey is not an election. It may be necessary and even desirable to ignore people's wants, as in the case of wasteful amounts of air conditioning or the desire of workers to hide from their supervisors. Some issues reveal irreconcilable conflicts between different user groups, as in the conflicting needs in a general hospital between patient privacy and staff surveillance. The outcome will typically be a compromise between conflicting pressures and trade-offs among the various design objectives, for example, a decision as to how much privacy will be traded for how much surveillance. Rarely will it be possible to give everybody what he or she requests. Those undertaking the UNA should make this clear to the respondents. However, the reverse attitude, that the survey is just a useless exercise with no practical value, must also be avoided. An employee who is interviewed as part of a UNA should be able to win a battle somewhere down the line, perhaps not in the overall design conception of the building or even in the arrangement of a floor or department, but perhaps in the desk area or in a choice between curtains and blinds. Even a minor victory can have great symbolic importance for the individual. At the very least it serves as an important tool for environmental or architectural education.

Most of the examples of the UNA that we have discussed so far have involved the public sector. There is nothing in this approach that excludes its use in private industry. Salespeople, clerical employees, and factory workers will benefit as much as public employees from involvement in design decisions. Corporations already make use of marketing analysis among potential customers. The same technology can be adapted for use with their own employees. This runs counter to management's customary reluctance to share decision-making with workers. This seems to be diminishing in the face of successful experiments in worker participation in Japan and Western Europe. As the gulf widens between those within the same large corporation who plan buildings and those who occupy them, it is inevitable that user participation in design decisions will occur. The risks of misfits between people and occupants will be too serious otherwise.

THE BUILDING PROGRAM

The translation of needs into design objectives is called the *building program*. The program links expressed user preferences to the site plan and to design elements. The building program is typically a written list of design criteria classified into different categories of users, activities, and areas. Before such a document is written, the statements of the different categories of users must be integrated and the costs and benefits of each option carefully considered. Building programmer Gerald Davis uses a systems analysis approach in which each element is seen as interacting with every other element.[7] The document focuses on decisions that must be made by the owner or client before the architect begins the drawings. These decisions concern issues such as land acquisition costs, energy use over the life cycle of the building, maintenance issues, possibilities for internal flexibility, for growth, and so on. Thus the program statement is not a set of drawings so much as statements about needs translated into design criteria transposed to a particular site. The development of a program statement is an accretive process, taking place over a period of time and involving consultations at many levels, to allow testing of tentative solutions before the final draft is written. The finished document will be a compromise between what people want and what the site, the budget, and top management will permit. The conscious effort to satisfy occupant needs may not result in everybody's being happy, but people should feel that their needs were seriously considered by the design team and that the result has been a fair compromise between the desires of individuals, the characteristics of the site, and the goals of the organization. The programmer does not simply hand a written document to the client and architect and then leave, but remains to see that the points made in the document are understood and considered as the design process unfolds.

Often the usable results of a needs analysis are general preferences for certain form and materials and a few specific concerns. The information on user needs will not be complete, since a project budget permits only a very small amount of time to go towards learning what the occupants want. The limitations of the data must be taken into account. The UNA approach does not mean that the occupants come up with the final plan. This is possible but not likely. Nor does it mean that when the designer begins looking through the stack of questionnaires, observations, photographs, and summaries of group discussions, the correct plan will suddenly leap to mind full blown. Again, this is possible but not likely. Putting the materials on site, economics, materials, safety, and energy together with the client's and the occupant's views and coming up with a fitting design will take time, effort, talent, sensitivity, and creativity. Occupant needs are formally considered as new constraints. Good designers in the past recognized the concerns of occupants but lacked systematic information on what the occupants wanted and how they used existing areas. In the short term, the new approach is more difficult since it includes additional information to be digested, translated, and applied.

In practice, there is considerable overlap between a needs analysis (UNA) and a post-occupancy evaluation (POE). The range and type of questions are often similar. People can be asked about their degree of satisfaction with their present facilities in order to identify unmet needs. The chief difference between the two approaches is the temporal orientation of the questions. *Evaluation* refers to what people already have while *needs analysis* refers to what people want. The two activities are also undertaken at different times in the design cycle; the UNA at the start of a project and the POE after the project is completed. The differences between the two techniques disappear when people are asked to indicate their desire for change. This transforms the POE into a needs analysis. On any given project, both UNAs and POEs from previous projects can be relevant. In planning an innovative building, statements about preferences may be more useful than assessment of previous structures. However in a common building type where many examples are in existence and have been evaluated, the POEs may be more relevant, although this does not rule out user participation, which can have important secondary benefits.

TABLE 4

Pioneer Schoolyard:
Translation of a Needs Analysis into Design Criteria

In 1982 landscape architecture instructor Mark Francis was asked by parents and teachers in an elementary school to prepare a design plan for the outside areas. Francis enlisted his students in conducting a needs analysis. Data collected over a two-week period included observations of the site to determine its features and how it was presently being used, interviews and in-class mapping exercises, questionnaires from parents of children at the school, and group discussions with the staff. The information was summarized in a report, which was the working document out of which the design alternatives were developed. These alternatives were presented to a meeting of parents, children, and teachers who selected one to be built by joint work parties over the coming summer months.

The translation involved extracting the major trends from the replies and applying them to general concepts of form, materials, site, and activities. There was agreement that the preferred materials for the yard were wood, turf, and vegetation (lots of shade for the hot valley climate). Disliked materials were concrete, steel, and plastic. Sand was favored by the young children, but some attention had to be given to staff concerns about mess. Many of the children also wanted water,

Continued

TABLE 4 (Continued)

but the teachers did not, and there were energy, resource, and safety issues to be considered. Regarding land form, some relief from the flatness of the valley was desired. This could take the form of mounds or recessed areas, but nothing too high (a concern of parents) or completely hidden from view (a concern of teachers). The use of topography to create barriers and markers was considered, since it was found that the children segregated themselves by age in their play activities. Other information concerned the types of activities engaged in by the children at each age level that would be useful in selecting equipment for the site. Primary usage of the outside areas occurred during 10-minute recesses and the 50-minute lunch break. Some possibilities for unobtrusive supervision by teachers needed to be included.

If user opinion were to be respected, the outside areas would *not* resemble the typical bare macadam schoolyard with fixed metal equipment and little or no vegetation. It would be the task of the design team to reduce potential conflicts either by eliminating controversial items, such as sand and water, or by designing safeguards to minimize the problems connected with them (keeping sand from being tracked inside the school or providing water without its being wasted or excessively messy). The final plan might include a controversial item, but at least the design team would be aware of potential resistance.

More than half the parents surveyed indicated a willingness to participate in the construction work during the summer months. Increased parental interest in the school was an important secondary benefit of the survey. Another benefit in negotiating between the different and often conflicting needs of potential occupants (in this case between children, parents, teachers, administrators, and custodians), is the time and expense saved during the review process, since the positions of different user groups are known in advance.

I LOVE HAWTHORNE EFFECTS

The effects of employee involvement are sometimes described as *Hawthorne effects.* This refers to studies of worker participation conducted in the relay assembly room of the Western Electric Company during the 1930s.[8] As a result of recommendations from the workers, conditions were improved and production rose accordingly. However, when most of the changes were removed, production stayed up. This created uncertainty as to whether the increased production was related to the physical changes or to the improvement in worker morale from their having been consulted. I will put aside the specific details of the Western Electric studies, which have been discussed extensively elsewhere (including the economic changes that occurred as the nation slipped more deeply into the Great Depression and increased the attractiveness of jobs for those workers still employed), and concentrate on the artificial distinction between "real effects" attributable to physical changes and "Hawthorne effects" resulting from improved morale. There is an adage in environmental research that one never changes a single variable at a time. I do not doubt that the workers interpreted the changes in working conditions as indicating that management was interested in their welfare and that this improved the workers' attitudes. This causal sequence was:

> *Consultation → Improved conditions →*
> *Raised morale → Increased production.*

Although there are other ways besides improved working conditions to raise morale, including higher wages and fringe benefits, the point remains that physical improvements represent one means among several by which management can demonstrate its interest in employee welfare. Whether the changes in production come about directly because of the physical changes or indirectly because of improved morale is beside the point. Social design can and should capitalize upon Hawthorne effects to justify capital investment in improvements.

During an evaluation of a small park that local people had helped design, Rachel Kaplan found that people enthusiastically supported the consultive process that had been pursued.[9] They felt it was important that this type of consultation continue. Attitudes were so positive that some people volunteered to help maintain the park! On a hospital renovation project, I found that the workers who laid the floor tiles preferred to create interesting patterns rather than spend all their time laying homogeneous floors. The head tile layer told me with some pride that it hadn't taken them any more time to create an attractive design than to lay it all in a single color. I am sure that the improved morale of the workers, who now saw a larger purpose to their efforts, played a significant role in this outcome.[10] I do not regard this as an accidental occurrence. Wherever possible, I have tried to capitalize on intangible motives. If attractive buildings are more profitable because employees believe that management cares about their welfare, I regard this as a solid argument for building attractive structures.

Designer Helge Olsen and his students constructed a soft classroom with the goal of increasing the amount of student discussion. Unlike the other classrooms, which contained tile floors, institutional chairs in straight rows, dull colors, and homogeneous fluorescent lighting, this one was carpeted, contained benches and cushions in a circular arrangement, and spot lighting that could be regulated by a rheostat. Students and faculty greatly preferred the new design and the amount of discussion increased.[11] Whenever I describe the findings, someone is likely to ask whether this might be a Hawthorne effect. I am willing to acknowledge that improved attitudes are probably involved in the increased discussion. Students and faculty feel more relaxed and comfortable in the carpeted room with lower lighting levels and this, combined with the ability of people to see one another, increases the amount of discussion. The dependent variable (increased discussion) is linked to *both* the independent variable (new layout) and an intervening variable (improved attitude), and any attempt to separate layout from attitude seems artificial. A building affects performance directly in terms of its functional characteristic and also indirectly through its effects on attitudes and feelings.

A major study of office workers conducted by Bosti, a well-known architectural research organization, which involved more than 10,000 office workers and executives, found that 81 percent felt excluded from design decisions about their work environment, 79 percent of these would have liked to participate in these decisions, and 72 percent of them felt some dissatisfaction because they were excluded. The privacy issue produced some startling levels of complaints: 98 percent of the workers surveyed said they could hear other people talking, 96 percent were able to hear phone conversations of other people, and 94 percent could hear other people's typewriters—not faintly in the distance, but clearly. Similar results were found in a survey of office workers by the Steelcase Office Equipment Company involving more than 1,000 office workers and 200 executives. There were gaps of as much as 54 percentage points between the number of office workers who have at least some say and those who consider it important to be involved. More than 70 percent of the workers surveyed complained about the comfort of their offices, and three quarters of those who complained said the discomfort reduced their job effectiveness. Given this high level of dissatisfaction, it would seem that soliciting worker participation would be profitable for a firm considering an office renovation or a move to new quarters.[12]

Hawthorne effects are important in the design process, but they do not by themselves justify a needs analysis. The requirement for a survey is the possibility of obtaining useful information. It is hypocritical and dishonest to undertake a survey without some commitment to using the results.[13] A needs analysis isolated from the design process is an empty and hypocritical gesture. The creation of Hawthorne effects is a valid *secondary* effect but not a valid primary goal of a needs analysis.

EXAMPLES

A. Two State Office Buildings

As an employee of the Space Management Division of the California General Services Administration, Yvonne Clearwater was assigned responsibility for conducting a UNA for two new state office buildings. Her first task was to inform the prospective occupants about what was happening and the options that were available to them. She prepared a brief pamphlet describing the planning process and

FIGURE 9 Informational handout distributed to employees prior to needs analysis.

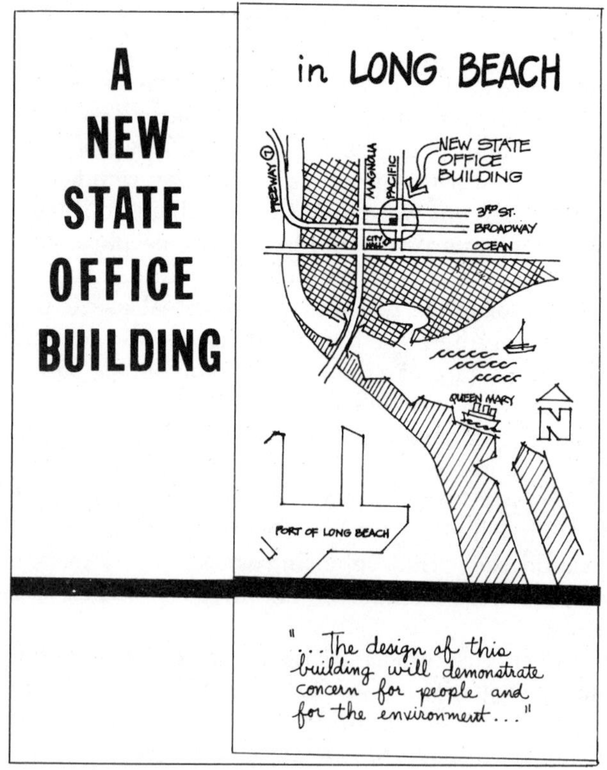

the goals of the needs analysis. The pamphlet included a sketch of the site (Figure 9) and listed the following goals:

Design of comfortable, functional offices
Flexibility and diversity of space use
Human-scale and noninstitutional work environment
Pleasant indoor/outdoor relationships
Energy-sensitive design with reduced reliance on nonrenewable resources
Varied materials and textures
Incorporation of appropriate artwork

The cost for 700 copies of the pamphlet, including the printing, material, and folding costs, was $31. A week after the pamphlet had been distributed, all the employees of the agencies projected to occupy the buildings received individual questionnaires (Figure 10).

FIGURE 10 First page of questionnaire used in needs analysis of two office buildings.

PLANNING SURVEY
NEW STATE OFFICE BUILDING

Please Leave Blank
Agency ________________ (1-2)
I.D. ________________ (3-5)
Job Cat. ________________ (7)

Name ________________

Job Title ________________ Unit ________________

Division ________________ Section ________________

The purpose of this survey is to assess the user needs and preferences of the future occupants of a new State Office Building.

Please indicate your answers to the following questions by placing an (X) in the appropriate boxes. You can ignore the key punch numbers printed beside the boxes. Space is provided for your comments on various items. Feel free to attach additional sheets for further comments.

Thank you for your cooperation. When you have completed this survey form,

please return to ________________________________

Continued

FIGURE 10 (Continued)

1. What are your tasks and responsibilities? ______________________

____

____

ADJACENCIES AND ACCESSIBILITY

2. Whom should you be located close to in order to perform your work?

Job Title	*Section/Unit*
______________	______________
______________	______________
______________	______________
______________	______________

3. If the following places were available to you in the new office building, how often would you use them?

Area	*Number of Times per Week*	
Cafeteria	______	(9)
Vending Area	______	(10)
Outside Eating Area	______	(11)
Coffee Area in Unit	______	(12)
Comments:	______________	

People were asked about their assigned duties and responsibilities, the need for public access, the need for adjacency to other work units, and the use of various facilities in the building, as well as requirements for storage space, office equipment, and filing and display areas. The survey was filled out by employees as they sat at their desks during their regular work hours. The cost of printing and assembling the questionnaires was $75 and a computer analysis of the results cost $817. In addition, the researcher made a hand-tabulation of the specific comments people wrote on their survey forms. These comments covered matters not included in the survey questions and also added a personal touch to the survey. The individual replies were hand-tabulated before the results were sent away for computer scoring.

Employees were questioned specifically as to their preferences for colors, materials, texture, and artwork. The instructions made clear that their preferences would be considered but it might not be possible to include everything that people wanted. Personal interviews were conducted with 20 managers and section heads. The information from these interviews was summarized by Clearwater and included in the report, which was completed four months after the study had been initiated. The only additional budget item was Clearwater's time as a space programmer for the period of the survey (during which she also worked on other projects), and the time spent by the employees in filling out questionnaires. These, of course, would have to be balanced against time that would be involved in doing the space planning without the UNA.

B. Military Dining Facilities

A team from the Construction Engineering Research Laboratory associated with the U.S. Army Corps of Engineers studied consumer attitudes at Air Force dining facilities. The survey combined an evaluation of existing dining halls with a user needs analysis of what people wanted. The latter took the form of asking military personnel to describe an ideal dining hall, including table size, wall color, flooring, ceiling height, and the like (Figure 11). Each respondent was also shown a color palette and asked to choose the most suitable colors. The results of the needs analysis were subsequently converted into design standards that were implemented at various Air Force bases and used to develop the profile of an ideal dining facility, which was described in two technical reports distributed to military food service officers, *Dining Facility Evaluation and Improvement Guide* and *Decor Guide for Enlisted Personnel Dining Facilities*.[14]

C. Army Family Housing

Another study conducted by the Construction Engineering Research Laboratory looked at housing for military families.[15] Figure 12 shows some of the illustrations intended to make the options more meaningful to the respondents.

FIGURE 11 Questions from a needs analysis of army dining facilities.

8. Below is a list of five WALL FINISHES. *Please select two of the finishes which you prefer for your dining hall.*
Place Xs in the boxes next to your two preferences.

- ☐ Smooth
- ☐ Textured Finish
- ☐ Wood Paneling

Continued

FIGURE 11 (Continued)

- ☐ Vinyl Wall Covering
- ☐ Ceramic Tile

9. Below is a list of four types of FLOORING. *Please select two of the types of flooring which you would prefer for your dining hall.*
Place X's in the boxes next to your two preferences.

- ☐ Vinyl Tile
- ☐ Hardwood
- ☐ Quarry (Clay) Tile
- ☐ Carpeting

10. If a LOUNGE AREA were provided in your dining hall, would you use it BEFORE YOUR MEAL? *Place an X in the box next to your answer.*

- ☐ Definitely Yes
- ☐ Probably Yes
- ☐ Maybe
- ☐ Probably No
- ☐ Definitely No

AFTER YOUR MEAL? *Place an X in the box next to your answer.*

- ☐ Definitely Yes
- ☐ Probably Yes
- ☐ Maybe
- ☐ Probably No
- ☐ Probably Yes

FIGURE 12 Illustrations used in needs analysis of army dependents' housing.

26. Which of the following closet door styles do you prefer? (*Circle one*)

a. Standard door

b. Bifold

c. Side-sliding

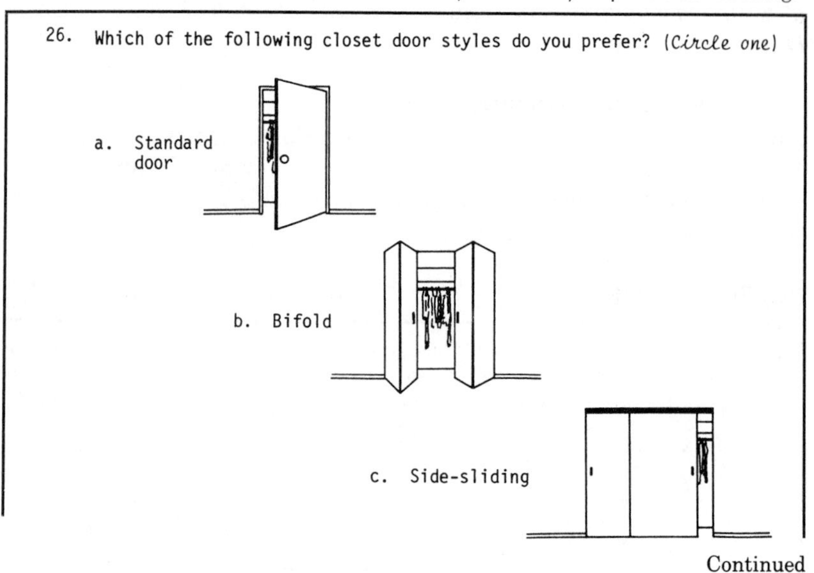

Continued

FIGURE 12 (Continued)

28. Which of the following kitchen-exhaust systems do you prefer? (*Circle one*)

a. Wall style

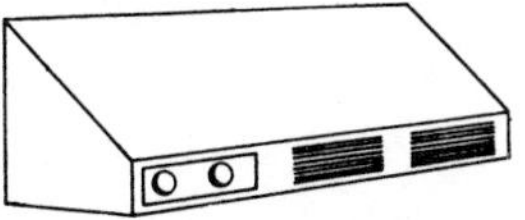

b. Hood style

29. Which of the following kitchen sink styles do you prefer? (*Circle one*)

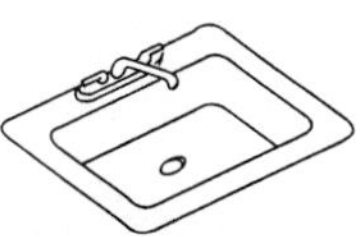

a. Single bowl

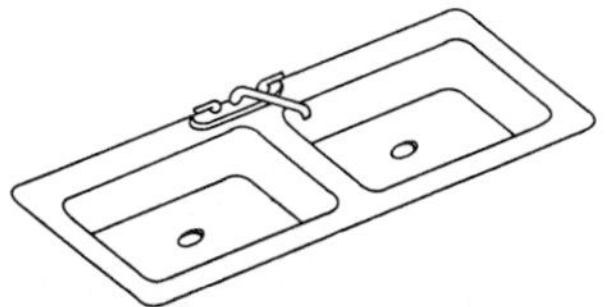

b. Double bowl

7

BRINGING IN A BEHAVIORAL CONSULTANT

The quickest and surest way to obtain social science input is to bring the social scientist into the planning sessions as a consultant. This can be done in a number of different ways, for example as a consultant to the architect, as consultant to the developer or owners, as consultant to public agencies, or as consultant to user or community groups. Each of these roles calls for somewhat different skills and involves different responsibilities. There is a long tradition for architectural offices to employ outside experts in transportation planning, communications, acoustics, and lighting. Social scientists can contribute information about occupant needs and wants. A major justification for their inclusion is the widening gulf between those who plan buildings and the actual users. Many projects are designed for occupants who are not known or available during the planning stage. Another justification for the use of behavioral consultants is the time and effort involved in extended discussions with occupants. A single meeting with a tenants' organization or neighborhood association will raise problems without developing solutions, and additional meetings may be precluded by cost and time constraints. The use of a consultant with experience on similar projects can sidestep some of these problems. Rapoport emphasizes that an outside consultant may see things more clearly than insiders who take things for granted.[1] It sometimes takes a trained outside observer to see what is significant.

The early dream that it would always be possible to involve residents directly in design decisions proved difficult to realize in practice. Often the occupants were not known before the project was completed, or if they did exist, the time frame and budget were so constrained that consultation was too expensive or time-consuming. When this occurs, information from previous research on similar buildings can sometimes substitute for direct contact with present or future occupants. This places social scientists in their customary role of researchers. If the project involved a convalescent home, information would be sought about the mobility of the elderly, their social activities, wheelchair access, lighting needs, and preferred colors. These are only a few of the behavioral issues that might arise during planning. The consultant would either have this information at his or her fingertips or know how to obtain it quickly and efficiently. This type of consultation involves not so much working with people as with written material in the library. In the long run, the appropriateness of this approach depends on the output of researchers. This is one reason why design research is so important.

The consultant's first task is to identify the client. On a large project this may not be easy. The best clue is the contract. No matter what people say, if you are being paid by X, then X is the client. You may never actually meet X, who has delegated the responsibility of working with you to someone else. This creates a murky relationship with a remote client (X) and a proximate agent (Y), with whom you must work on a routine basis. David Canter has found that his most productive relationships occurred when he was introduced to the design team by the person paying the bills. This experience can be contrasted with that of another colleague, who found himself consultant to a staff member of an interior design firm that was the subcontractor to an architect's office that was the prime contractor. The psychologist felt that his input was coming in at too low a level to have any effect. This makes contract negotiations a critical step in consultation, in which consultants define for whom they are working, the nature of their responsibilities, timetables, deadlines, and so on.

There are also intangible roles that a behavioral scientist can fill on the design team. I have served as a catalyst or translator in discussions when it became evident that the client was not comprehending what the engineers and the architects were saying and vice versa. Occasionally my role has been to serve as a counterweight to another consultant. This occurred in a hospital renovation plan for a state health department. All of the design team had visited the existing buildings. The engineers were tremendously impressed with the concrete warehouse-like areas because they were structurally sound and earthquake-proof, but very negative to several wood-framed cottages that were used to house patients in special programs. These views ran totally counter to the opinions of the hospital staff and patients, who disliked the concrete barns as much as they appreciated the small cottages. My role was to provide data on the views of the staff and patients that could balance the findings of the engineers. The eventual recommendations represented a compromise between structural integrity and user satisfaction. This happened only because there was someone available to represent the occupants.

Frequently a behavioral consultant is not in a position to provide specific information relevant to a particular project so much as a body of accumulated experience that allows, on the basis of a look at the plans or even conceptual diagrams, the formulation of questions about the ways in which the proposed design might operate, given certain assumptions about the way that people will use particular spaces. The consultant becomes useful by asking the right questions and making educated guesses about possible outcomes based on assumptions derived from the programming document. This amounts to a *behavioral reading* of planning documents, which is akin to a reading that someone versed in mechanical engineering or heating control systems might provide. This type of consultation is much more valuable when conducted at the conceptual phases of design rather than the point at which contract drawings have been developed. By that time changes become so expensive that the architects are probably looking less for new information than just for confirmation that what they are doing is correct. Social designers can contribute most effectively in the design process if they are brought in before all the major decisions have been made.

At the completion of a project on which social scientists have participated, it may be difficult to specify the exact nature and extent of their contribution. When I questioned Neal Deasy, one of the first practicing architects to collaborate with social scientists, about how much of the information obtained from sociologist Tom Lasswell he was able to incorporate into the design, he could offer only a general reply. He believed that the information from Lasswell was helpful in writing program statements and setting priorities, but that it was difficult to isolate this input from the total decision-making process. This is probably a characteristic of many good team arrangements, in which decisions are made by consensus with each person's having made some contribution.

Very little has been written about the problems in generalizing findings from one setting to another. Design work is similar to clinical practice in using a custom approach. Each community is unique with a special and never-to-be-duplicated combination of tangible and intangible features. The convalescent home that is suitable for one town may not be appropriate for another 20 miles away. The second community may, in fact, prefer home visits by a public health worker to residential services. The factors that distinguish between the two solutions can be identified and explained if one wants to invest the time and effort, just as individual motives can be identified and explained, but they are difficult to predict in advance.

The fact that a solution must be customized does not mean that it is arbitrary or neglectful of what has been tried elsewhere. Researchers have found that the elderly need a higher level of illumination and are more troubled by glare than younger people are. Older people are also likely to have hearing problems and fears of slipping and falling. The team designing a convalescent home should take these considerations into account. It is one thing to ignore previous findings because they are judged to be irrelevant and another to disregard them out of ignorance. There will always be a transfer of information from previous projects and this can be modified to fit current conditions.

Psychologists entered into design projects in any way they could—as invited guests to observe the action and occasionally to whisper in the ears of their hosts, as hired hands to assist with the chores, or to satisfy their own curiosity. Some had to pry open a lock or break down a door in order to enter. A few used friendship or family ties to infiltrate. There are still too many unanswered questions to specify at this time the ideal role for social scientists on design projects. Some who have served as consultants believe that they have had more impact when working directly for the client than when working for the architect. Since the architect was responsible to the client, the recommendations had to be approved by the client in any event. Psychologist Gary Winkel studied space use at Bellevue Hospital in New York City. Hospital officials were so impressed with his report that they brought Winkel into the selection process for the architect who would make the changes. In this reversal of traditional roles, the environmental psychologist became the architect's client. This model of working as a consultant to the client or becoming part of the client organization may have more influence upon architectural practice in the long run than for social scientists' serving as consultants to architects.

Another approach that has been rarely used up to now is for researchers to attempt to influence policy by working with agencies and boards that set zoning rules, building codes, earthquake standards, fire and life safety codes, airport noise rules, and so on. William Whyte, who has spent several decades observing people's use of space in downtown areas, has been influential in modifying zoning regulations to reward builders for including pedestrian amenities in their plans.[2] Whyte was hired as a consultant to city governments and planning departments to help in writing new zoning regulations. The developer who creates a plaza or park with adequate sitting space might be allowed to put up an extra floor or use additional ground area for commercial activity. Architect Michael Durkin is currently studying how people respond in earthquakes, and psychologist David Canter is studying reactions during fires. The issue is not being approached in terms of danger and panic in the abstract, but in terms of people-place relationships. What aspects of a building improve orientation in the event of a disaster? How can panic be minimized when the alarms sound? The full potential for design researchers in developing building regulations is just now being explored. In the future, one would hope that building codes would be based in part on the findings of design research.

The different time worlds of the behavioral consultant and the practitioner pose a serious obstacle during first-time collaboration. Once they have worked together on several projects, these problems are likely to be resolved. Some of the improvement will be a result of eliminating those consultants unwilling to follow tight deadlines, and those designers unwilling to educate consultants as to what is needed. A useful consultant's report is (a) pertinent to the situation of the building's occupants, (b) written in a form that is comprehensible to the designers, and (c) available when important decisions are made.

In a rational world it should be sufficient that a consultant's report is relevant, comprehensible, and timely for it to be used. Unfortunately this is not a rational world and utility does not guarantee use. The situation may call for advocacy. On most projects a consultant is not only an information gatherer and report writer, but a spokesperson for certain recommendations and solutions. The ability to present recommendations persuasively is an important part of the consultant's job.

Many people do not want to have their lives complicated by new information. A colleague who became involved in a six-figure school renovation project found that all the funds were going to be used to improve staff areas and nothing would be done for students. Suggestions for reversing the priorities were not well received. Neither his client (the architect) nor the liaison group from the school district (administrators) wanted to hear about student concerns. There was a need for someone to assume the role of consumer advocate, but there was no forum in which the presentation could be made to a receptive audience. Consumer advocates will be listened to and heeded only when they have a strong constituency behind them. Building occupants are unorganized and sometimes unknown prior to a structure's completion. Representing phantoms does not provide adequate leverage for a consumer advocate in the design process.

Getting one's ideas accepted requires preliminary discussions to learn what the client is *willing to hear*. Note that "willing to hear" is different from "wants to hear," since there is a tolerance range of acceptable divergence from expectations and desires. Informal discussion will reveal that the client regards some issues as nonnegotiable and outside the consultant's purview. When the consultant believes that the client should hear these unwelcome messages anyway, there is an obvious dilemma. One can press ahead and speak the truth, even though the information is unwanted and unlikely to change anyone's mind. Occasionally it will be possible to make an end run and find someone else in authority who is willing to hear information rejected by the client. This is a dangerous practice and should be avoided unless absolutely necessary. Going behind a client's back is certain to generate bad feelings and jeopardize future collaboration. One alternative is to introduce the information through informal channels. Without putting anything in writing, the consultant passes along impressions and recommendations privately to those people who might be able to make use of them. Called in to advise an organization whose president does not want to hear about certain matters, the consultant might informally speak to a sympathetic vice president at the conclusion of the visit. The conversation might run something like this, "Look, I have been brought in to evaluate X and have conveyed my report to the boss. In the course of my visits, I found other things that need looking into. There is a good indication that people in Y aren't terribly happy with the way the project is going and the people in Z feel that no one is listening to them. I thought you would like to know these things since you have expressed an interest in the well-being of Y and Z. Here are some ways that I think the problems might be remedied. . . ." This approach recognizes the value of informal channels of communication.

There are times when people's preferences have to be put aside for valid reasons, as in the case of insufficient funds or resources. Corporate employees may want air conditioning because that is what they have been led to expect from their previous quarters. A behavioral consultant may assign this desire for air conditioning a lower priority than energy conservation, and instead of working as a consumer advocate on behalf of the employees who want air conditioning, work instead with the architect to gain acceptance for a climatically responsive building whose occupants will be allowed to dress for the seasons. An enlightened advocate does not blindly represent consumer opinion. An important part of the organized consumer movement has been education. The input of uninformed consumers may be worse than no input at all. Behavioral consultants who have failed to do a proper job of educating future occupants may find themselves not only lacking a constituency but opposed by the constituency they want to represent.

Architect Neal Deasy remains optimistic about the possibilities of a social scientist as an independent consultant. However, Deasy believes that such an individual would have to be "exceptionally aggressive and a hard seller." There is a market out there for behavioral consultation, but it needs to be clearly defined to attract clients. Psychologists cannot simply sit under their diplomas and wait for architects to call. Methods are being developed for bringing together potential clients and consultants. For some time, architects had wondered aloud how they could locate a behavioral consultant in their locality who could contribute to a specific project. Behavioral scientists had sometimes expressed an interest in working with architects only to be rebuffed by firms that did not want their services. Rapport between the two professions is being improved through professional associations such as the Environmental Design Research Association (EDRA), which brings together, in annual meetings, behavioral scientists interested in design with architects interested in behavioral sciences.[3] Proceedings of the sessions are published and a quarterly newsletter is circulated. Perhaps the best way for a social scientist to become known in a specialty area is to do research and publish the results. Most of my consulting experiences began with someone reading an article or book I had written.

Brief consultations have a hit-and-run quality that can be frustrating in the absence of feedback. I have provided single-day consultation on projects as varied as a rapid transit system, a research laboratory, a bank, and a university library. The dangers of brief consultation were most apparent in the library project, where I was given no documents to read in advance. The architect believed that if I were asked to read anything about the project, he would have to increase my fee. We met for one day in a conference room. Throughout the entire morning, I assumed we were talking about a new main library for the campus. At lunch I learned that we were talking about a specialized undergraduate reading room. My comments during the morning about journal storage and use of periodicals, which are not major considerations for undergraduates, were largely irrelevant. Luckily I had the afternoon to undo the damage. I can imagine that the whole day might have passed without my realizing that I was thinking about the wrong kind of library.

Consultants should be aware of the feedback systems operating in the fields in which they give advice. I have come to accept with resignation the fact that people to whom I have sent detailed evaluations are unlikely to respond even when they have found the information useful. I'm not sure that I understand the source of this reluctance to communicate, yet it seems more the rule than the exception. If building evaluation can be seen as a feedback system for designers, then those who conduct the evaluations need some feedback from architects, owners, and occupants. It is not so much expressions of thanks or gratitude that are required, but guidance and direction as to what information is useful and what is not.

Social scientists who have been engaged in design consultation have wondered aloud if their input made any difference. On a large-scale project in which many people have participated, it is difficult to determine individual contributions. I am not aware of many instances in other fields (including law, medicine, and business) where the worth of any type of consultant has been conclusively demonstrated. This may be an area where value must be assumed on the basis of internal logic and agreement among the other participants that behavioral concepts are relevant and useful.

If I were to look back on all those projects in which I was personally involved, the most satisfying by far has been bikeway design. The main reason for this higher level of satisfaction has been the availability of my own community as a laboratory. I was part of an interdisciplinary team of engineers, landscape designers, behavioral scientists, and ordinary citizens that made the city a model for mixed transportation, including adequate provision for cyclists. Urban planners and city officials from around the world have visited us to see what was done. My contribution was in research, evaluation, documentation, and dissemination. The largest share of credit belongs to the city public works director, David Pelz, who implemented many of the findings along with his own good ideas so that we could all learn which ones worked and which ones did not before the ideas were borrowed by other communities. Such experiences have convinced me of the value of local research in which the researcher is part of the community in which changes are made, and thus has the opportunity to guide, evaluate, and redesign proposed changes.

STATE-OF-THE-ART VOLUMES

A century ago it was possible for a sensitive observer who had extensive experience with a particular type of building to write a definitive and useful book. Sheriff John Howard's *The State of the Prisons in England and Wales, etc.*[4] provided the pattern for prison construction throughout the Victorian era in England, and Thomas Kirkbride's *On the Construction, Organization, and General Arrangement of Hospitals for the Insane*[5] influenced more than a century of mental hospital construction in the United States. Today there are too many variations of prisons and mental hospitals for a single individual to know them all. There are specialized facilities for children and adults, halfway houses, community residences, and institutions for the criminally insane that are part prison and part hospital. The information has become exceedingly complex and difficult to locate and synthesize.

A useful format for summarizing available information on a

replicable design problem is the state-of-the-art volume. The topic can be as narrow as concert hall acoustics or as broad as all aspects of park design. The author's task is to critically evaluate what has been done previously and develop the implications for future construction. Preparing a book of this type means visiting many buildings and wading through a vast amount of written material. The volume must be more than a collection of photographs, building plans, or renderings. Such collections can be helpful in expanding image banks and providing visual information on the ways that others have approached the same problem. However, without evaluational data, including some indication of the success of the projects, such compendia would not qualify as a state-of-the-art volume.

I have a large collection of photographic slides of bicycle paths that I have loaned to communities planning for bicycle transportation. However, without evaluational data, the slides are incomplete and misleading. Some of them illustrate traffic arrangements that were not successful. One city used low concrete barriers to keep parked cars away from the sidewalk and to create an interior bike lane between the curb and the parking lane. The appearance is very appealing to anyone who sees it. Unfortunately, this layout is extremely dangerous for the cyclist at intersections, since neither drivers nor cyclists are aware of one another's presence due to the visual obstruction caused by parked cars. Eventually the city removed the concrete barriers and switched to painted white lines between the parked cars and the traffic, which increased the visibility for both drivers and cyclists. It is important for me to retain pictures of the concrete barriers in my collection as an illustration of something that did *not* work, but without an accompanying text, the viewer would not know this. A state-of-the-art volume must coordinate pictures with words—not merely any words, but critical analyses and evaluations of systems as they operate.

A state-of-the-art report is also more than a study of a single building. By its nature, the study of a single instance stresses the uniqueness of the project, including site, materials, sponsors, users, politics, and cost. A project may fail because of political decisions or economic changes outside the client's control. This might be the main conclusion of a case study but it would not have much prominence in a count of all similar projects that did not fall victim to these particular problems. Case studies often deal with unusual projects such as the Boston City Hall or a playground for blind children. A state-of-the-art work is also more than a compilation of case studies.

A good state-of-the-art volume contains a list of references and citations. Some periodicals refuse to include references as a matter of editorial policy. It is presumed that footnotes and citations "clutter up" the text and bore the reader. This is a very shortsighted approach. References link the present with the past and provide opportunities for the motivated reader to explore the issue further. It is intensely frustrating to see facts and figures mentioned without knowing where they came from or where more detailed information can be obtained.

Many design studies will be out of print and difficult to obtain. There are also likely to be references to unpublished documents, such as the program statement issued by a planning firm. The only possible course of action available to the interested reader is to write directly to the firm. There is no guarantee that this will produce a response. Even worse than getting no reply is to receive an enormous mimeographed report lacking useful information. However, this will not be known until the report has been examined directly. The prevalence of unpublished documents is one justification for accessible state-of-the-art volumes.

Unlike most glossy coffee table books that are long on pictures, short on text, and deal with unusual and noteworthy buildings, state-of-the-art volumes will contain as much text as pictures, and deal mostly with ordinary buildings. The 1980 catalog of Architectural Press in Great Britain includes such titles as *Hotels, Motels, and Condominiums; Open-Office Planning,* and *Prison Architecture.* Aaron and Elaine Cohen, an architect-social scientist team, do an excellent job of synthesizing behavioral factors and physical design in libraries.[6] Their book is a useful reference source for anyone planning a new library or renovating an old one. However the recommendations will be outdated as new findings emerge, thus creating a niche for new editions. Because it is a published work, a state-of-the-art volume will always be somewhat behind current work. Computerized information storage and retrieval of building evaluations is technically feasible at the present time. Start-up costs would probably be higher than a system based on mimeographed or photocopy sheets mailed out to a list of subscribers, but the long-run economies would be significant. A data base consisting of building evaluations screened and set into a standardized format at a central location would provide useful information quickly and efficiently about particular building types of design elements.

The three following accounts illustrate the range of projects on which social scientists have worked.[7] They are neither the best nor the worst of such experiences. All three authors had worked with planners and architects before and after the particular projects described here.

EXAMPLES

A. David Canter, Surrey, England. A Cross-Channel Tunnel and a Games Area

Every few years someone explores the possibility of building a tunnel under the English Channel from England to France. One such plan called for a tunnel for trains which would carry both passengers and their automobiles. This would require two large terminals, one in England and one in France, to which people would drive their cars to be loaded onto the train. A large architectural firm in England was called upon to provide, among other things, plans for the British terminal. As chance would have it, one of the founding partners of the architectural office had been on the advisory board of my research unit, and during a discussion of our mutual activities we spoke about the involvement of his firm in the design of the terminal and the possible contribution that an environmental psychologist might make to the project. Thus my involvement began at a very high level in the architectural firm. My meetings with the architect responsible for the project were relaxed and open from the very beginning. The architect always seemed keen to see how I could help, at times declaring the opportunity to talk with me as analogous to a regular visit to a therapist!

My consulting took the form of a day-long visit to the architectural office about once every three weeks. I would be told about new developments in the project, problems encountered, and possibilities being explored, and I was able to discuss with the individuals responsible for different aspects of the operation the various approaches that they were considering.

Since the firm was still exploring the feasibility of the project, it was not considered of value for them to commission me to carry out substantive research. I did conduct a few interviews as well as read all the background material I could find, but my role at this stage was really to provide an outside perspective on the project. Three aspects of my involvement that had some impact on the planning process are worth noting. Early in our discussions, I described the terminal as being a context in which people who initially were in a free state under their own control and driving on a motorway would change to being parts of a controlled, structured line of cars on a train. The terminal would work as a funnel so that people could change from a free to a controlled state. The architectural office took this conception very seriously and proposed to use landscaping and general planning to slowly lead people into increasingly channeled lanes between grass mounds that became higher and were eventually covered with trees in a large, funnel-shaped plan.

The second idea that seemed to influence the design came out of discussions with people who were asked to imagine themselves as users of the terminal. People all seemed to expect that there would be a large entrance towards which they would be moving. They would use this entrance to judge how far they were from the goal. It was important to uncover this concept because technical considerations required that the tunnel entrance (the actual hole in the ground) be located a few miles from the terminal itself. The designers therefore took it upon themselves to create a focal landmark for the project, a tower in the center, which would provide a clearly visible anchor point by which passengers could measure their progress.

These two aspects of my involvement could be seen as positive contributions deriving from the experiences I had in turning ideas (sets of concepts) into words, which the architects could then convert into a design and models. The next issue we faced in this project shows how the same type of contribution can be valuable in a negative sense. A sophisticated computer system was expected to count people, issue tickets, and give directions to the appropriate platform for the next train. As a psychologist with experience in putting people through complex experimental procedures, I was immediately struck by the certainty that not everyone would politely do as they were requested. I posed the question of whether some "awkward customers" could introduce perturbation into the system that could bring it to a halt. This did not seem an especially profound question, but the next time I visited the design office, I found they had modified the computer system so that the presence of "awkward people" would not jam up the entire operation.

Regarding my participation in the project, the architect pointed out that everyone else he spoke to—the client, the engineers, the building economists, and the other designers—all had particular professional perspectives and "axes to grind." He saw me as someone with no particular special view except that of the users. He could therefore discuss all the pros and cons in an open way and gain fresh insights. This seemed especially necessary because of the unusual nature of the project. The architect considered me "insurance" that the views of the users would be included. The project showed me that conceptual input at the early stage of design can be even more valuable than the detailed statements that come much later. I also felt that I was able to take an overview of the project only because of my prior environmental research experience.

GAMES AREA

Our invitation for this project came in an unusual manner. The managing director of a recreational firm, Playtime, Ltd., was discussing the design of a games area with his architect. At one point he turned to the architect and said, "How can you design this without knowing who you are designing for? Do you have an environmental psychologist on your staff?" The architect had never heard of such a creature but agreed to seek a suitable candidate. That search brought him to interview me. He subsequently presented a report to Playtime, Ltd., listing the people he had met and recommended that I and my colleague, Ian Griffits, be employed to work with him. Thus from the start we worked closely with the architect and his partners while still having the active support and encouragement of the client. In one sense the designers knew that the client wanted them to listen to us.

As part of our involvement, we analyzed and summarized Playtime, Ltd.'s own records. We were able to show them aspects of their clientele and operation which ran counter to their own preconceptions. For example, it was a common belief within the organization that the majority of customers lived locally, but by examining a random sample of customer addresses and preparing this in a chart, we were able to show them that this was not true.

We also undertook behavioral mapping of the existing recreational centers. We charted where people were located at various times. Even when the facility was crowded, there were areas that were under-utilized. We were able to point out that the existing design created spaces that were unattractive. We proposed a redesign of equipment and new layouts that would help to increase utilization during peak periods.

We also made suggestions regarding background illustrations and graphics in the recreational facilities. It was current practice to have these as neutral as possible, yet one of our findings was that people using the equipment wanted to choose different areas with different ambiences to suit their moods. Great variation was disliked because of the focus on the recreational activity itself. It occurred to us that a distinct but subtle difference in ambience could be created by the selection of illustrations in any given locale. The architect had originally proposed something like this, but without the justification of the proposal, it had been discarded. With our more reasoned account of what was to be achieved and why, the idea gained a more sympathetic hearing from the client.

As a condition of our involvement, we were not allowed to interview any customers. We could interview staff but we could only observe customers unobtrusively. This left unanswered questions, such as why people came to these places and what they thought they got out of being there. We therefore embarked on detective work to fill in this central piece of the jigsaw puzzle using all the other information we could collect. This led us to produce specific recommendations for design and layout that would facilitate the desired type of staff-customer interactions.

In summary, here is a list of roles that come up during these and a number of other consulting experiences:

- Therapist—outside listener
- Verbalizer—exploring implicit ideas
- Organizer—putting actions in sequence
- Advisor—providing expert opinion
- Researcher—collecting and analyzing data
- Executive—acting on and making decisions
- Facilitator—providing a way for people to communicate with one another.

B. Frank Becker, Ithaca, New York, Branch Banks

"We're involved in the expansion and renovation of branch banks. We heard about you from _____. Your work sounds relevant to what we are doing. Can you come down to New York City and meet with some of our people, look over what we are doing, and share your thoughts with us about some proposals?"

"Sure."

I flew to New York City from Ithaca on the morning flight and went directly to the design office on Park Avenue. It was exciting to be at a Park Avenue office for my first paid consultation.

I met the principals of the firm and learned that they were consultants to other consultants for the bank. So I was a consultant to a consultant to a consultant for the bank. They showed me plans of several different interior arrangements and asked me what I thought. I felt on the spot, since I did not have a lot of information to share. Neither then nor now is there a body of behavioral studies on banks as there is a body of work on housing or schools. I suggested that if they wanted to get more informed judgment about the possible impact of the proposed designs, some kind of study, however qualitative and informal, should be done. I suggested a "data blitz" in which several people would descend on a site and furiously collect data for a brief period, and then move on. This could be done in urban and suburban banks, those that offered full service and partial features, and that had special distinguishing architectural or other features. The head of the firm thought this was a good idea. He asked me how much I charged and how long the study would take. I named a fee I thought was outrageously high. He agreed to it immediately, and asked me to send in a brief proposal. I did, and shortly after they accepted it and the project was underway in style.

I hired two architecture graduate students who had been working with me on another project. Based on some preliminary observation in local banks, we produced an environmental rating scale for customers and for employees (different forms) and an observation checklist for customer and employee behavior in lines, conferences, teller transactions, and other settings. The intent of these procedures was to help us develop informed judgment, not do a scientific study.

We worked hard for our money. Arriving at a bank, I contacted the manager, who was expecting us. After explaining what we would do, one of us interviewed the manager, another began the customer interviews, and the other observed various components of the branch operation. Each of us did more than a single activity, so that we could discuss and confirm whether our individual impressions were shared by the other team members. We covered 20 banks in a three-day period.

Returning to Ithaca, we worked frantically for the next 20 days preparing a final report. I did most of the writing, including the verbal description of the findings and design recommendations. The architects developed the findings and recommendations into visual design criteria. These were subjected to a lengthy critique and then revised. The final report was ready within two weeks. We found that the backstage employee areas needed more attention than the public areas. Customers select a bank because it is convenient and offers services they value, not because of its interior appearance, so long as this falls within the common range of rather mediocre bank interiors. Customers are more concerned with the demeanor of bank employees than the physical environment. The employees, however, were concerned about their working environment and we felt that improvements in their physical surroundings could translate into improved customer-employee relations.

We sent the report to one of the design principals, and then made an oral report to a high level bank representative and a representative from the consulting firm which had hired the consulting firm which had hired us. The response was generally favorable. Several weeks later, the design firm made a presentation to the bank in which material from our report, including our drawings, comprised almost two-thirds of the final presentation.

I have no regrets about my participation. In addition to the glamor and excitement of New York City, and making money to boot, the consultation was stimulating. I learned something about decision-making in complex organizations, about different types of consultation, something about banks that has made my own personal use of banks more interesting, and gained knowledge of what behavioral science can and cannot contribute to design and to social change. It was also an opportunity to develop a good working relationship with the architects on my team. We complemented each other extremely well, both in terms of what we observed in the bank and what we contributed to the final report. Their drawings summarized the verbal recommendations beautifully, and contributed significantly to the visual excitement and legitimacy the report had for the designers. This kind of working relationship helped me to differentiate between consulting and collaboration. The bank study was consultation. Its potential for stimulating a more responsive design was limited by the brief duration and intensity of a relationship in which an outsider presses for change without having the time to build trust and confidence, to take small steps, to involve many people.

C. The Author, Fiji Island Resort

The design team for a prospective island resort in Fiji was a fascinating amalgam of practicality and idealism. It consisted of six individuals in the fullest sense of the term: a hard-nosed engineer who wanted to do things the engineer's way—going out in the field and obtaining information to set the limits and constraints within which the rest of us would work, an intuitive visual-minded architect who was continually straining to return to his drawing board and evolve a personal design concept, another architect who was the team leader and the formal representative of the client's interest, a town planner trained as an architect, a graphic artist, and I, whose job was described as "human ecologist." I was on the team so that we could "do something better than the Los Angeles developer" who kept calling the client on the phone offering to buy the island and turn it into another Waikiki Beach.

Before going to the five-day design session on the island, I read as much as I could about local culture and ecology. I learned that there wasn't much of a natural ecology on the island to be preserved. Animals had been introduced by European settlers a century earlier and had dramatically altered the flora and fauna. There were, however, several archeological sites which had been examined by the curator of the Fiji Museum. I spent a week visiting hotels on the main island to learn something about the behavior and attitudes of the potential visitors to the resort. I stayed in seven hotels in seven days and visited half a dozen more, probably a record for Fiji.

Later on, during the design sessions, I acted as a facilitator in breaking down communication barriers and making sure that people understood what others were saying. This seemed a particularly necessary role since people from different fields and cultures were involved. I found the days prior to our departure for the island—where the various team members interacted socially—helped to improve communication when we reached the island.

There were problems of team leadership and of identifying the client. Throughout the sessions, I took the position that the architect who had brought us together and would be paying us was the client, and the rest of the team were his consultants. However, when the owners of the island and several government ministers visited the site to listen to our recommendations, this perception of the situation became difficult to maintain. Rather than the rest of us being the architect's consultants, all of us became a single team attempting to advise a client.

The major contribution I made pertained to housing for the native workers. The architect's conception had been dominated by his image of a traditional native village. I pointed out that this was appropriate for groups with a common kinship system and a shared culture, but totally inappropriate for natives recruited from various islands who did not share the same cultural assumptions or live in a subsistence economy. An urban form with small shops and service buildings would be far more suitable for this work force based on the type of workers who would be employed at the resort.

I also contributed to the discussions on how the resort could be made to blend in with the island's topography by using natural colors found on the island, by limiting the height of buildings to the palm tree line, and by ensuring some separation between different hotels that might share common facilities. The entire project was tremendously exhilarating because of the physical beauty and unfamiliarity of the setting, the divergent backgrounds and interests of the team members, and the tight deadlines under which we operated.

DIRECT PARTICIPATION OF OCCUPANTS

The preceding two chapters described how occupant needs can be brought into the design process through surveys (Chapter 6) and through the use of consultants as consumer advocates for the occupants (Chapter 7). The most direct means of including user opinion is to have the occupants themselves present during the design sessions. This is the most challenging, difficult, frustrating, and rewarding application of social design principles. It can upset the delicate balance among those presently involved in the design process and raise critical issues of authority and expertise. Issues surrounding citizen involvement have implications far beyond architecture and urban planning to the very basis of how a society operates. The goals of this chapter are to define the nature of user participation in design, specify various levels from token involvement to full control, indicate its costs and benefits, and provide some examples of how it has been achieved.

Above all, this approach is not practicable for all projects. Especially when new construction is involved, the potential occupants may not exist in a real sense. Many commercial buildings are constructed by large architectural firms and financed by major banks without specific clients in mind. Leasing is done by a rental agency after final approval of the design has been obtained. College students who plan a new residence hall will not be the ones to reside in it. There may be a delay of ten years between the initial conception and the final opening of the buildings for use. The student population will have turned over several times in the interim. Furthermore, the residence hall will be used for several decades and student needs are likely to change during that period.

The priority assigned to different categories of occupants must be considered. The employees in a government office may represent only a small proportion of the people who will come into contact with the building, but they will spend long periods there, unlike casual visitors whose trips to the facility are infrequent and brief. Those who administer and maintain the facility will also want a voice in its design.

All this should give pause to the idea that direct participation of potential occupants is an all-encompassing solution in design work. It is a splendid ideal but attainment of even an approximation requires deliberate planning and hard work. Only on a handful of projects can this approach be tried out in a relatively pure form. It is no coincidence that most of the participatory designs of modern buildings have been sponsored and paid for by outside agencies, rather than by architects, clients, or occupants.

VERNACULAR ARCHITECTURE

In less-developed lands, user-generated design is the rule. Families plan and construct their dwellings using available materials and a widely shared technology. The whole tribe or village joins together to construct common buildings. Tribal involvement provides shelter and strengthens social bonds. A lack of participation in constructing buildings indicates social breakdown. With shared images of what buildings, interiors, and public spaces should be like, and an accessible technology using available materials, there is no need for designated architects or builders. Community participation is a way of life, thereby giving the environment qualities of stability, evolution, and movement no different in its characteristics from other parts of nature.[1] The success of this approach in meeting shelter needs in less-developed nations is well accepted by international aid agencies who have learned that they cannot impose a particular (Western) model throughout the world.

The social design approach has little to offer in a primitive society dealing with problems in its immediate environment. Designers, clients, and occupants are one and the same. There is no communication gulf to be bridged, no need for user surveys or building evaluation, so long as the essential tribal structure and environment remain intact. The methods of social design will be helpful if discontinuous changes occur, such as a multinational corporation's constructing a large mine or mill nearby, or a paved road from the national capital coming into the village. These types of changes will bring new problems so rapidly that the tribal mechanisms for dealing with problems will be overwhelmed. Some type of formal citizen participation may be necessary to cope with the new developments, whose magnitude may dwarf the village, in order to preserve local culture. Such participation might undermine the existing social organization, in which decisions had previously been made by a chief or group of elders, but this will probably be a less serious disruption than will result from the unforeseen changes.

Nor will social design approaches be necessary in small villages or towns with a division of labor in construction, but where there is direct contact between occupants and builders. Amos Rapoport calls this type of construction *preindustrial vernacular*.[2]

The term *vernacular* refers to the shared assumptions present in local culture. In a small village, where a family can hire carpenters, masons, and other tradespeople to construct a dwelling, the ongoing dialogue between the two parties would render unnecessary any formal survey of user needs. Vernacular architecture is specific to particular cultures. In traditional situations, each little area—each valley, each district, each province, and often each town—has a certain uniqueness that makes it different from others.[3] Clients and occupants are one and the same, and have direct contact with builders, and all operate under shared cultural assumptions. Rapoport sums up the characteristics of vernacular architecture as working with the site and microclimate; respect for other people and *their* houses and hence for the total environment; lack of abstract theoretical or aesthetic pretentions (including a lack of interest in novelty for its own sake), and working within an idiom with variations taking place within a given order.[4]

Professional architects and planners entered upon the scene only late in Western history. Initially they were brought in by kings and clergy to design important public buildings, while the construction of mundane buildings was left to tradition and the labor of ordinary citizens. Vestiges of this dual arrangement still remain. There is a tendency to restrict the term "architecture" to major structures designed by professionals, and ignore the ordinary tract houses, supermarkets, local stores, gas stations, and drive-ins in which most people live, shop, and work. In this view, the phrase "vernacular architecture" is a contradiction in terms. If a building is "vernacular" (that is, built according to shared cultural assumptions without professional assistance), it is not architecture.

The vernacular process of direct contact between occupants and builders fell into disuse for a number of reasons. The technology and cost of large structures lay beyond the resources of individuals. This created the need for professionals and outside agencies, putting a gulf between owners and occupants, and another gulf between designers and occupants. The loss of a shared value system and common view of the world also weakened the role of tradition in regulating buildings. The spirit of cooperation diminished, and people lost respect for the rights of their neighbors, and ultimately for the rights of society as a whole. This necessitated explicit codes, regulations, and zoning rules.[5]

There are still traces of the early ideals in many of the current applications of user-generated design in Western nations. As distinct from high-style buildings based on the architect's quest for novelty and self-expression and the inherent properties of form, social design favors forms and materials connected with culture and geography. Preference for the vernacular can explain why social design did not produce a distinctive style or motif. Social design is more concerned with the relationship between individual elements, how they are connected, than in the appearance of single elements set apart, the so-called jewelry approach of architecture. The current attitude toward user participation is part of an evolutionary spiral moving upwards and around, so that we are back at the same place as earlier generations in acknowledging the importance of participation, but affected by the social and technological changes that have occurred during the intervening period. We have returned home but home itself has changed.[6] Although primitive societies may represent the ideal application of user-generated design, it is not clear how well they can serve as a model for user-generated design in advanced Western nations.

THEORY OF LOOSE PARTS

Visualizing the environment as a totality which must be planned overall at one time makes user participation unnecessary and even harmful. Occupants of a building can contribute meaningful suggestions and know their own needs regarding only a small part of a larger structure. User participation rests on the assumption that the environment is composed of small pieces or units that can be planned separately, but must fit together into a larger meaningful whole. This concept has been described by designer Simon Nicholson as a *theory of loose parts.*[7] As an illustration, Nicholson takes an analogy, not from art or architecture, but from gastronomy. In the process of creating a meal, the ingredients are chosen and assembled by someone, experimented with, evaluated, added to, or subtracted from, and the collection of pieces evolves into a series of dishes that are then consumed in part or in whole. Each dish is a loose part in a meal, and the meal is a loose part in a day, which itself may be a loose part in another system, such as a work schedule. This is seen as a prototype of the way that designs should be made, that is, by taking a set of loose parts and assembling them in some way. There is an overall purpose in the operation that governs how the pieces are fit together and in what order, but the final product is evolutionary and bottom-up, coming out of available materials, technology, and labor, rather than top-down, from the vision of a designer or client.

Social organization is included among the parts. In designing a school, the curriculum, the composition of the student body, and the areas of instruction covered would be among the pieces considered. This can take the design team far afield from what is ordinarily thought of as architecture. It may be that certain parts (physical or social) are fixed and unresisting, and are more properly viewed as constraints than loose parts, but this judgment emerges from the planning process and is consciously accepted rather than assumed in advance. Design therefore becomes the process of assembling the parts to "find a place for things." The parts come first; the vision of the whole comes later. The imposition of an overall image upon a landscape, with all the parts taking their character from that image, is seen more properly in the domain of sculpture or monument-building than architecture. There is nothing in the loose-parts theory that rules out comprehensive planning, order, or symmetry, but this flows from the subsystems. A street or plaza is designed out of the loose parts to fit those parts. The totality is more than the individual pieces, but it takes its character from them.

Nicholson considers the degree of inventiveness and creativity in an environment to be directly proportionate to the number, kind, and distribution of parts. Loose parts also allow for modification in a setting as conditions change. Even a perfect fit between the final plan and the present occupants is likely to be outmoded as the occupants change. The Village Homes development, discussed later in this chapter, illustrates how loose-fitting parts can exist harmoniously with an overall conception of an energy-conserving development. It may seem paradoxical, but Village Homes has been internationally acclaimed both for its overall plan and its participatory planning methods. There are few communities in America where the residents have played a more active role in design, construction, maintenance, and policy-making. There is no contradiction between comprehensive planning and user participation when the planning stems from a conception of residents as active and involved. Nor is there any inconsistency between an ecological perspective and a theory of loose parts. In both cases the environment is conceived of, not as an amorphous, undifferentiated blob, but as networks of interrelated systems.

Flexibility is the bridge between the theory of loose parts and vernacular architecture. Vernacular buildings have the ability of being added to, subtracted from, or changed, without losing their identity. They have a very stable equilibrium. They are extremely flexible without losing their basic character. On the other hand, "high-style buildings" do not accept modification. If one small item is changed, the whole configuration may look like nonsense.[8] This is one reason why high-style designers are so insistent that nothing about the building be altered without their expressed permission.

HUMAN SCALE

The need for participatory methods increases with the size and complexity of projects. The larger the scale, the more likely occupants are to become passive onlookers to the work of outside professionals and hired workers. The smaller the project, the more feasible it is for people to share in the planning and construction. The importance of scale explains why participatory methods are better developed in city planning than in architecture or interior design. While many schools of urban planning teach courses in community decision-making and advocacy planning, there are very few architectural schools that teach courses in participatory design. Yet the size and scope of some individual buildings, such as factories, community colleges, or prisons, may be larger than those of a neighborhood redevelopment, if not in the amount of space, at least in the number of occupants.

Scale will also determine the proportion of occupants that can be involved. On a small project, all of the residents can share in the planning process. When the project exceeds a certain size, limits will have to be set on the number of participants. Beyond a certain number, it is unlikely that additional representatives will contribute new information. In such cases, opportunities should be left for others to express their views on the project, either directly or indirectly through public meetings, letters, or site visits, so that they do not feel that their opinions are unwanted.

Participatory methods tend to produce design pitched at a human scale. People generally don't design things for their own use that are going to dwarf their lives, homes, and neighborhoods. The scale difference between participatory and formalistic designs is evident in the comparison between user-generated parks and those designed by landscape professionals. A formalistic park is designed as a totality, often with a rigid geometry involving large grassy areas with keep-off-the-grass signs. The spaces are intended to set off public buildings. They are important as symbols and showplaces for governments. They are tourist centers attracting visitors from over a wide region.

When local citizens design community parks, the results are very different. They don't create a smaller version of the formal park, with its empty spaces and clean geometry. Rather they think in terms of functional areas to be used and enjoyed by nearby residents. The park is not seen as a magnet for a region; it is not a tourist attraction. That is the last thing in the minds of local residents. Often the park is integrated into the neighborhood so as to seem territorial and keep away outsiders. Recycled materials and local labor are likely to be used. Even without consciously knowing the principles of defensible space (Chapter 3), neighborhood residents tend to design open spaces that are both territorial and have good visual surveillance.

Scale is one determinant of the appropriateness of participation. Territoriality is another. Planners of a project contained entirely within the bounds of a particular neighborhood should solicit the opinions of residents. When a project crosses boundary lines or involves spaces without permanent occupants, such as a national park, participatory design would not be practicable. Some other method for obtaining user input, such as a needs analysis or behavioral consultation, will have to substitute for direct participation. Overall planning of an urban mass transit system will need to be done on a centralized basis by professionals, working with government officials. Yet the design of the individual stations and the planning of routes and service facilities should involve neighborhoods.

TYPES OF PARTICIPATION

Turner classifies environmental decision-making according to whether it occurs before, during, or after construction.[9] Other writers distinguish between participation according to whether it affects the private domain of the individual or public spaces. Becker identifies five degrees of user participation in environmental design: (1) the creation of forms and objects themselves; (2) the selection and arrangement of forms that are provided; (3) a choice between alternative plans that are complete in themselves; (4) providing information to a designer who draws a plan; and (5) no consultation or choice.[10]

The two examples presented at the end of this chapter illustrate the wide range of occupant participation that is possible. Example A describes a residential development that encouraged people to be active throughout, even to the point of designing and constructing their own homes and joining the homeowners' association afterwards. Example B involves a government agency that allowed employees a few options regarding office furniture in a new building. These options were not typically available to lower-level government workers. On the surface, these two examples have little in common. The only shared feature is that the potential occupants were allowed some input into the planning process. This diversity illustrates why it is so difficult to draw up rules for including users in the planning process. Perhaps the most that can be done is to define those conditions most likely to lead to successful participation:

1. A client (individual, agency, or corporation) who consciously seeks to promote the well-being and morale of the occupants.

2. Designers with big ears willing to listen to the occupants. Satisfaction of occupant needs takes precedence over ego.

3. Occupants willing to commit themselves to the hard work of learning enough to contribute effectively to the planning process. The same individuals should participate throughout the planning sessions and represent legitimate constituencies of users. If they feel that they represent only themselves, they may be hesitant to express their opinions or argue for specific measures.

4. Sufficient time and freedom from pressure for designers and occupants to become acquainted, learn each other's languages, assimilate available information, and explore various alternatives.

5. Information aids and tools that are flexible and manipulable to increase the realism of the project and to move it swiftly and deftly from the verbal to the visual realm. Some public "involvement" is incredibly uninvolving. Discussions never seem to get anywhere, and information is presented in an unengaging fashion.[11] The types of blueprints, plans, and documents that will interest professionals may have little meaning or significance to lay people, even those who have had direct experience in a building similar to one being planned. Some translation is necessary to make the graphic and technical information meaningful to nonprofessionals so that they can offer informed opinions.

There will be times when the line between needs analysis and user participation is difficult to draw. When a space planner interviews a prospective occupant regarding equipment or space needs, it is needs analysis. If the same occupant attends planning sessions and takes part in discussions, that is participation. The difference is not in the amount spoken by the individual (who presumably will speak proportionately more when being interviewed than at a large meeting), but in the format of the sessions. The interview is intended to elicit information from one person to be used by another to come up with a suitable plan. Participatory design means that the entire group does the planning. Needs analysis is pre-design, and part of the programming phase; participation is part of design work in which decisions are made. There will be instances in which the two activities merge, as in the case in which some occupants are interviewed while others take part in the planning sessions.

Let us consider a commercial chemical laboratory whose future occupants will be scientists, technicians, and support personnel. Needs analysis involves interviews with representatives of each user class in their existing work spaces to determine their space and facility needs. The information from the interviews is taken back to the architect's office where it is summarized, collated, and included in the programming documents, to be reviewed later by the full design team. It is the occupant's task merely to supply the information that others (that is, design professionals and their consultants) will use. Participation takes a very different form and would occur over various stages of the project. It could range from token to full participation and involve varying numbers and types of users. Token participation might involve one scientist and one technician appointed by management to attend a few early planning sessions without having had access to cost figures, planning documents, or other significant items of information. A great deal of so-called participation is unfortunately of this token variety. Those attending sessions do not feel that they have any legitimacy in representing a constituency and little understanding of what is taking place. The danger is that the presence of a few occupants at the early sessions, without their having been briefed earlier or understanding what is going on, can be used to justify and excuse inadequate planning.

Much of the demand for user participation in environmental decisions began as a protest against something. People in the path of a planned freeway or adjacent to a new commercial development found they had to organize in order to be heard and effective. From the standpoint of the residents, it was clearly better to be involved in the decisions at the outset than to attempt to react after all decisions had been made. From the standpoint of the planners, it was better to hear potential objections early in the planning process than later. Once it became clear that local residents had potential political power and were able to use it, it was in everyone's interest to include them in the planning process. Only when they were voiceless and powerless was it feasible to exclude them from decisions. This is still the situation in regard to architecture of many large buildings, where the residents are unorganized, voiceless, and powerless.

The need for user participation remains throughout the life cycle of a building. Without this, the benefits of participation are denied to all but a few occupants. In the furnishing of the Seattle branch offices of the FAA (described later in this chapter), the initial occupants had their choice of furnishings but employees hired later did not. Not unexpectedly, it turned out that the people who began working in the building after the furniture decisions had been made were less satisfied with the outcome than were people who had been involved in the planning. To deal with this problem, we had recommended that the agency set up a furniture pool containing surplus items. If a new employee did not like the furniture provided, he or she could visit the furniture pool and select new furniture from available items. This might not be as satisfactory as choosing brand-new items from a catalog, but would provide the employee with some feeling of control over the immediate work station.

Attempts by occupants to alter the physical environment to suit their individual needs are often discussed under the heading of *personalization.*[12] Architectural contracts may be written to preclude any changes by the users, to the extent that even such minor items as posters on office walls, employees' bringing in their own plants, or housing project tenants' using some of the exterior space for gardens, are prohibited. Such unpopular rules, which decrease occupants' feelings of belonging, self-worth, and control over the environment, are not likely to result from participatory planning methods.

One critical objection to participation is that it will inevitably produce chaos. People will not know what they want, different user groups will make conflicting demands, there will not be an overall theme or harmony in design, and so on. In response to this objection, Alexander, et al., argue that user input will not result in chaos when there are shared principles.[13] They cite the harmony inherent in vernacular architecture in support of their position.[14]

Another general objection is that many of the present occupants are not going to occupy the new facility and therefore have no moral right to impose their own ideas on future generations of residents. The similarity between existing and future occupants will always be a matter of degree. The solution is to select for the planning process individuals as similar as possible to future tenants. Often the best candidates will be found among present occupants. When this is not the case, some alternative procedure, such as post-occupancy evaluation of identical buildings elsewhere, can be tried.

USER EDUCATION

If they are to contribute effectively to the planning process, potential occupants must acquire knowledge about the project, its goals, costs, constraints, and the nature of the planning process. They must have some idea of time and budget allocations, their own role and those of the architects, interior designers, communications consultants, and all the varied cast of characters they will encounter. They will probably lack this knowledge initially, but they will have to learn as the planning proceeds. All too often the person reaches peak effectiveness just about the time that the planning winds down. Such an individual will be a tremendous resource for the next project, if there is one.

The educational lessons acquired can be divided into those connected primarily with (a) technical details regarding the setting (number of work stations, employees, machines, degree of telephone access, and the like), (b) information regarding the social organization of the facility, and (c) information about the design process. The initial planning session can be made educational to bring the occupants up to the point where they can contribute effectively to the discussions. This does not mean that everyone must acquire the same level of understanding about all phases of the project. There will still be some specialization among the participants, but there will be a general comprehension of goals, methods, and constraints.

People involved in participatory design projects comment spontaneously on the amount of learning that takes place. The specific lessons are not always pleasant, as in the realization of how little power the occupants possess in relation to city authorities, banks, corporations, labor unions, and so on. Planning the layout and quality of space for a neighborhood or institution makes people aware of how power is distributed and how decisions are made. Even something as minor as the placement of litter receptacles brings to one's awareness considerations of aesthetics, attitudes toward authority, civic pride, and the feasibility of recycling. There is probably no better way to achieve environmental education than to involve residents in environmental decision-making. In an evaluation of user-generated parks in New York City, it was found that those local residents who had been active in creating community gardens, playing fields, and parks felt that this increased their own attachment to the neighborhood and their confidence in the area, and also increased their skills in relation to the urban landscape.[15] There is an old Chinese proverb:

I hear, and I forget
I see, and I remember
I do, and I understand.[16]

Pre-design workshops and simulation games can be used with people who will subsequently take part in design sessions.[17] This requires a commitment of time and effort, but the hope is that an intensive learning experience can bring participants up to the point where they will be able to contribute effectively to the deliberations. Lawrence Halprin and Ann Halprin pioneered the use of experiential workshops as educational tools.[18] The Halprins devote considerable time to developing nonverbal sensory awareness and the sense of movement through space. Phyllis Hackett and I tried workshops that were more verbal and didactic. One week-end session involved teachers and administrators from a school district that was going to design a new school. We met in one of the existing schools, which became a natural laboratory in which we could move things around and experience different arrangements of space. Another workshop was held in a community hospital about to embark on an extensive renovation program. The sessions combined sensory awareness with group discussions on the effects of hospital environment on patients and staff.[19]

It is frustrating for me to acknowledge that we have no idea how these workshops affected the final outcome in these two cases. No request for evaluation was forthcoming from the client in either facility. This reflects the fragmentary application of social design techniques on actual projects. Project A has a pre-design workshop (hooray!); Project B has a needs analysis (whoopee!); Project C uses a behavioral science consultant (great idea!); and Project D has a post-occupancy evaluation (may the sky rain dolphins!). There have been few opportunities to combine these varied techniques in a coherent manner and see how they mesh. It is possible that behavioral science consultation will be unnecessary when the actual users take part in planning sessions. A more likely possibility is that the role of the behavioral scientist will shift from needs analysis (conducting surveys) to facilitation and analysis during the planning sessions. In any event, there has been little opportunity to understand how user participation fits in with other social design activities.

Participatory design requires more time than more traditional methods of consultation and requires a client sympathetic to this approach. There will probably be few projects on which full-fledged user participation at all stages of the project can be implemented, yet this still remains a standard by which existing projects can be judged, and a realistic option on a small number of projects where conditions are appropriate. Full-fledged participatory design may be far more significant as an ideal than as a reality. If designers are encouraged to soar to heights of imagination in conceiving of physical form, they should also be able to do this with the planning process itself. All designers should be exposed to the dream of full participation even though they may never be able to realize it.

ADVANTAGES

Participation in design helps satisfy people's needs to create and control, and is a way of producing environments responsive to occupant needs.[20] It brings people together to talk about common problems, which may be extremely beneficial in a divided community or a large bureaucratic organization in which people do not know one another. Participation in design establishes connections between people and their physical surroundings and creates a sense of community among those engaged in the planning process. It provides an opportunity for people to learn how their own space and material needs intersect with those of other individuals. Thus employees in one department or residents of a neighborhood will be able to see how their activities mesh with those of other departments or neighborhoods, and how this all fits together into larger systems. Participation is a means of consciously bringing about "Hawthorne effects." The decision to allow employees to participate in design decisions will demonstrate some degree of management concern. This will be appreciated by the employees, and may also have public relations value to outside agencies, such as banks, potential investors, government agencies, and trade unions.

Becker studied the effects of user participation in the design of college dormitories and the renovation of a general hospital. In the dormitories, he found a connection between the amount of student input in the original designs of a facility and the level of satisfaction among currently enrolled students, both with the dormitory as a whole and with their individual rooms. The study of the general hospital involved a comparison of three nursing units, one of which was renovated with input from the nursing staff and patients. The input came from interviews, questionnaires, and behavioral observations. The renovation changed usage patterns in the nursing unit and resulted in an increase in conversation, especially for visitors and patients during the evening visiting hours. The renovated areas were much more positively evaluated by both patients and nursing staff. There was an improvement in mood and morale among staff, patients, and visitors. People reported that the bright appearance of rooms and corridors cheered them up, and that they were more satisfied with the quality of health care at the hospital. The changes made the hospital appear modern and progressive.

A report on another hospital renovation project can help explain the basis for the improved morale. The headline of the newspaper article describing the project was, "Placerville nurses help design new hospital wing." In the next sentence, the administrators describe the 27,000 square foot addition as a "nurses' special." Staff nurses who were heavily involved in design and selection of equipment for the facility conducted tours on opening day. The director of nursing explained, "The nurses were real involved in the planning and preparation, so they kind of feel it's their wing. . . . Too many hospitals are designed by people who haven't stayed in them."[21] One can imagine the pride that the staff nurses must feel in reading such accounts. They were able to make their views felt during the planning sessions and received formal praise afterwards. This is very different from the situation in most hospital renovation projects where nurses (other than the superintendent of nursing) play no role in the planning. One can almost hear the nurses enthusiastically referring to "our building." I will admit to similar feelings about buildings to which I contributed as a consultant. Even when I cannot document exactly what my contribution to the project has been, I still feel some personal identification with the outcome.

The two examples that follow illustrate that participation can occur in different times and amounts on different projects. In Village Homes, prospective residents were involved in the planning of their individual homes and in the development of community spaces (playground, open spaces, community gardens) throughout the life of the project. In the FAA project, office workers were able to select their individual office furniture from among a range of available options and decide on layout within the work group. Although the amount and type of participation in each case was limited, the fact of having a voice in planning decisions was a source of considerable satisfaction to the occupants.

EXAMPLES

A. Village Homes

The Village Homes development in Davis, California, was planned with a high degree of user participation. This was due to a strong commitment to social design on the part of the developers, Mike and Judy Corbett.[22] Visiting Village Homes today, the most striking external design features are the steeply sloped roofs containing solar collectors. The interiors of the houses are interesting, with large dark cylinders storing heated water, skylights and lofts, and an airiness suited to solar heating and natural ventilation. The streets are narrower than in conventional developments to minimize heat radiation during the hot months and water run-off during the rainy season. Bicycle and pedestrian paths are separate from the roadway. Parking is off-street in driveways and shared parking bays. Front yards are small and the saved space has been consolidated into common gardens and play areas for each cul-de-sac. The cluster arrangement of houses is intended to provide good "defensible space" in the form of adequate surveillance and territorial feelings among residents of each cluster. People who desire a private outdoor area can fence in the back yard. Most leave the back yards unfenced for additional garden space or common open space. Instead of a concrete drainage trough, a natural creekbed is exposed to carry away the heavy winter rains. Commercial orchards, the income from which goes directly to the homeowners' association, are scattered throughout the development.

The decentralist philosophy of Village Homes encourages diversity and innovation within the units themselves. Many of the homeowners participated actively during both the design and construction. Some designed and built their houses entirely by themselves. Others had the developer do everything, but received a discount for doing the painting and the clean-up themselves. There was much more room for individual expression and innovation on this project than in the typical housing development, despite the consensual energy-saving features. Many residents continue to be actively involved in the management and evaluation of the community. Ac-

FIGURE 13 Group work party in Village Homes Development. (Photo by Michael Corbett)

FIGURE 14 Orchards maintained by the Homeowners' Association are interspersed with houses in the Village Homes Development.

tivities include the planning and construction of a new playground, buildings for the sale of vegetables and fruits from gardens and orchards maintained by the homeowners' association, and so on.

Village Homes represents an interesting combination of top-down innovation in the overall conception of an energy-saving community and bottom-up innovation in the design of the individual units and the outside areas. The potential for creative expression takes on a different form in this system than it does in top-down design, where it is likely to be dominated by a particular style that comes out of the experiences of the designer and client rather than from the occupants. One of the key factors in the success of the project has been the continued presence of the developers, Mike and Judy Corbett, on the site. Having them reside in the development puts them in touch with problems that arise, and allows them to shape the evolution and fine tuning of the project. The physical presence of landscape architect Lawrence Halprin has contributed to the success of Sea Ranch, an environmentally-conscious planned community along California's North Coast. This project began more than 20 years ago and is still in process. The presence of the designers is a healthy corrective to the loss of contact with completed projects that often occurs.

The Corbetts are presently working on plans for an energy-efficient small city, originally named Patwin after the previous Native-American occupants of the area. Patwin is intended to make optimal use of passive and active solar equipment, wind, and biomass conversion; to encourage minimum reliance on the automobile; to foster local small industry and small agriculture; to promote bicycle and pedestrian distances and locally owned shops and services, to institute townhall governance, and to limit the size of the town to several thousand inhabitants, with the town site surrounded by productive agriculture and biomass-producing areas. Unlike other New Towns, this will be more than a bedroom community. A specific requirement will be that the city not be built on prime agricultural land, but rather use Class 3 or Class 4 land and attempt to reclaim it through composting and other methods. Should Patwin ever be built, the architecture will be vernacular, human scale, designed to provide for community and for privacy when desired, and will avoid both the crowding of the cities and the isolation of the suburbs. There will be strict design controls as there are presently in Village Homes, but these will be the joint effort of the developers and residents. There will be compromises and constraints throughout the planning and development with local government officials, bankers, and the residents who will view some things differently than do the developers.

B. FAA Regional Headquarters

Architect Sam Sloan coordinated a project in which employees in the Seattle Regional Headquarters of the Federal Aviation Administration (FAA) were able to select their own office furniture and plan office layout. This represented a major departure from prevailing practices in the federal service where such matters were decided by those in authority. Since both the Seattle and Los Angeles branches of the FAA were scheduled to move into new buildings at about the same time, the client for the project, the General Services Administration, agreed with architect Sloan's proposal to involve employees in the design process in Seattle, while leaving the Los Angeles office as a control condition where traditional methods of space planning would be followed.

The project team consisted of two architects, a space planner, an interior designer, and myself, an environmental psychologist. We had no control over the exterior or the mechanical systems, which were the responsibility of the prime architectural contractor. Our first task was to inform the employees in Seattle that the project was about to take place and what their part in it would be. Our previous experience in similar projects had taught us several important lessons. We rejected the idea of asking employees to select furniture sight unseen from a glossy catalog. Giving people choices among items about which they knew little would create the

FIGURE 15 Many office employees feel oppressed by drab institutional surroundings.

FIGURE 16 Employee participation produced a heterogeneous homey quality appreciated by the workers at the Seattle FAA Regional Headquarters.

illusion of consultation without the substance. Rather than asking the employees what they wanted, we showed them the available options and let them try them out and discuss them with their fellow workers in order to make informed and considered choices. A furniture catalog was assembled through joint consultation with agency management. Sample items were obtained from suppliers and assembled in a vacant warehouse. A mock-up office was visited by 380 Seattle employees who tried out the furniture and made their selections in terms of style, color, and materials. Employees were encouraged to sit in the chairs, write at the desks, work at the tables, insert items in the file cabinets—and share their reactions with their fellows. Each worker was allowed to choose a combination of items within a price range established at his or her grade level within the agency. This requirement had been set by the agency. However, within the price range, the employee could choose any combination of available items, including novel combinations based on individual work needs.

The group discussions that followed the warehouse visits were an important part of the planning process. Employees who had no prior role in selecting office furnishings were often unfamiliar with the criteria to be used in making choices. Seeing their coworkers sitting in the chairs and at the desks and listening to their comments were part of an educational process. Discussions also helped to mesh one employee's choices with another's. Employees were good-natured during their visits to the warehouse, but many were skeptical that anything would come of it. They had become so accustomed to having their work stations planned for them that the idea of individual choice seemed alien.

Several months following the move into the new buildings, surveys by the research team were made in Los Angeles and Seattle. The Seattle workers were more satisfied with their building and work areas than were the Los Angeles employees. In addition, those Seattle employees who had been most active in the planning were more satisfied with the outcome than were those who had been less active. It is noteworthy that the Los Angeles building has been given repeated awards by the American Institute of Architects while the Seattle building received no recognition. One member of the AIA jury justified his denial of an award to the Seattle building on the basis of its "residential quality" and "lack of discipline and control of the interiors," which was what the employees liked the most about it. This reflects the well-documented differences in preference between architects and occupants.[23] The Seattle layout was decentralized, modest, and personal, with the individual work station at its core. The office had an unplanned quality to it, as the total arrangement evolved from the sum of the individual decisions. The director of the Seattle office admitted that many visitors are surprised that this is a federal facility. Employees in both locations rated their satisfaction with their job performance before and after the move into the new building. There was no change in the level of satisfaction in the Los Angeles office and a 7 percent improvement in rated job performance in the Seattle office.[24]

POST-OCCUPANCY EVALUATION (POE)

Twenty years ago the architectural profession was dominated by an attitude of "never look back." Once a building was finished, the architect moved on to the next project and then only returned for the open house or to check on an occasional leaky roof. This reluctance to return to occupied buildings stemmed from both architectural contracts that involved no additional remuneration once the building was completed and the architect's fear that the tenants would spoil or demean the building. Some design firms attempted to guard against the latter possibility by writing into the contract a stipulation that no changes could be made without the architect's expressed permission.

This detachment from occupied buildings has diminished during the past two decades with the advent of post-occupancy evaluation, or POE. While still practiced by only a small number of firms, POE is becoming better known within the design professions and among social scientists interested in these issues. There is increasing recognition that systematic examination of working buildings can provide useful information. At one time the American Institute of Architects sponsored awards based on juries making their decisions from glossy photographs or drawings. It was not uncommon for a major building to win awards before it was open for use. Now the policy is that at least one member of the jury should visit the site and talk to occupants of each building being considered. I'm not sure how fully this policy is being implemented, but it shows some recognition of the need to take into account occupant views before deciding whether or not a building is meritorious. POE differs from eyeball inspection in that it uses standardized procedures for gathering information and some effort is made to obtain representative incidents or samples of behavior.

POE can encompass something as large as a housing project or as small as a single item, such as lighting, color, or furniture. Interior designer Walter Kleeman evaluated chairs for the Federal Aviation Administration (FAA).[1] Because of the stress air controllers experience on the job, the FAA wanted to try to make their working conditions as pleasant as possible. It was felt that since air controllers spend most of their days sitting down, comfortable furniture might make their jobs easier. Kleeman undertook a mail survey among 10 percent of the 25,000 air controllers on the FAA list.

He also visited airports in the United States and Switzerland to talk with air controllers. His study found that many aspects of chair design needed improvement.

Kantrowitz and Nordhaus evaluated a housing project built by the Albuquerque, New Mexico Housing Authority.[2] An interesting twist to their study was that they returned afterwards to see what effects the POE had had on the client agency and the residents. The initial POE had been extensive, involving attitude surveys with half of the households, interviews with public officials, in-depth interviews with tenants, site inspections, and behavioral mapping of resident activities. The information was transmitted to the agency in the form of a detailed technical report with a brief executive summary. The major finding in the study concerned the residents' desire for greater territorial definition of the site. This was important to the housing authority, which had previously regarded fencing and landscaping as frills to be cut from the budget at the first sign of a money problem. As a result of the POE, the housing authority contracted with a landscape architecture firm to work with the tenants on a site improvement program. All exterior spaces were clearly identified as either public or private. Private spaces were landscaped and fenced with the tenants being responsible for their maintenance. Tenants could select plants and fencing materials. The POE increased the credibility of the housing authority with city officials and with the tenants, who felt that the POE and subsequent actions were persuasive evidence that the housing authority was making a concerted effort to upgrade the project and deal with community problems. The recommendations in the POE have been converted into a developers' handbook, to be used by the housing authority in planning additional housing units.

Some evaluations conducted by students or faculty are freed from ordinary cost constraints. For a Ph.D. thesis, Toni Farrenkopf studied how a university department was affected by its move to a new building,[3] and Yvonne Clearwater documented the move of a government agency from closed-cubicle offices into an open plan layout.[4] Each of these studies took several years to complete and involved careful multi-method assessment. Their investigations would be difficult to justify under the budget constraints of architectural practice, but it is important to have such examples available to show what can be done in POE when the time, facilities, and trained personnel are available.

At the other end of the continuum are those brief follow-up studies bootlegged by design offices under existing project budgets. While they may not meet academic standards of method and research design, they can be very important in improving practice.

The difference between academic and practical evaluations is one of degree rather than kind. Adding a detailed follow-up to an early POE may convert what was essentially a practical evaluation into one that will have academic currency and perhaps even theoretical significance.

There has been a tendency for practitioners to question the value of academic evaluations because they are so costly, time-consuming, cumbersome, and seemingly unrelated to the realities of practice. On the other hand, there is a tendency for academics to dismiss the informal assessment procedures used by architectural firms. Some degree of mutual tolerance is required so that the field can profit both from academic evaluation, the goal of which is to advance theory, and brief evaluations, the goal of which is to advance practice.

In all branches of applied social science, techniques for rapid assessment exist alongside more careful, time-consuming procedures. There are brief paper-and-pencil tests for screening intelligence that can be given by an untrained examiner to a group of people in 30 minutes. There are also individual I.Q. tests that require several hours of a trained examiner's time. Each type of assessment has its utility, but one should not confuse results from one with results from the other. I should add that the total scores from the two types of tests tend to be highly related. The main difference between them is not in the total score or level, but in the special applications of individual tests and the amount of information that can be extracted from them.

I came across an interesting account of a branch of anthropology known as "salvage archeology," which specializes in quick examinations of field sites:

> *Fredrickson had only three months to complete his excavation before the bulldozers moved in. He would scramble in with a field crew to retrieve what data he could. It was, by any definition, a salvage job, and in the vaunted halls of academe few terms are more blasphemous than salvage archeology. But Fredrickson felt, and often proved, that salvage archeology did not have to be done with relaxed standards. It just had to be done fast and under a lot of pressure.*[5]

The intense interest in the physical support systems necessary for video display terminals (VDTs) in offices illustrates the tight deadlines involved in evaluation. "Right now there is approximately 1 VDT for every ten office workers at every level," declared Amy Wohl, president of Advanced Office Concepts Corporation, a Philadelphia firm that helps businesses plan their automation. "In less than 10 years there will be one terminal for every worker. If we spend the next 5 years doing studies on what should be done, it will be too late. In a year or two, too much money will have been committed."[6] That evaluation should parallel implementation may not be the most rational model, but it seems the only approach for the headlong rush into the new office technology. Commercial firms are not willing to wait until the results are in. They want their share of the current market or they fear they will be squeezed out. Evaluators must be prepared to adapt their timetables to commercial deadlines.

Evaluation is fundamentally different from design in its time coordinates. Evaluation deals with the past and present, design with the future. Psychologists were first brought into the design process with the hope that they could predict the effects of buildings before they were constructed. Typically the psychologist would be shown a set of plans or drawings and asked how the building would affect the occupants. On a lesser scale, a psychologist would be asked to recommend one of several options, such as shared or separate entrances. Design education contains a significant amount of futurism. Students are given assignments to plan cities under plexiglass domes and buildings on water. The reward system of architectural practice reinforces this future orientation and discourages a concern with the past. There are financial *dis*incentives in making post-occupancy evaluations in which the costs must be borne out of the architect's fixed commission.

Psychologists, on the other hand, are given little encouragement to dream about the future. Their training and practice dwell upon the past as a guide to the present. Most therapy involves mucking about in earlier events to identify sources of problems; basic research is the slow accumulation of knowledge through minor variations on existing themes. There would be value in exposing behavioral science students to design problems with a future dimension. I do not mean physical design problems so much as social design problems. Students might be asked to plan a community support system to deal with child abuse or a cityscape that would promote interest and excitement without increasing visual clutter. Such exercises flow naturally out of the subject matter of psychological theory and research, but, unlike most training exercises, they look ahead. A reconciliation between what F. Scott Fitzgerald described as "the contradiction between the dead hand of the past and the high intentions of the future"[7] is possible through the critical evaluation of earlier projects as a guide to new construction.

If building evaluation is to improve design practice, information from previous projects must be fed forward to guide new construction. This requires standardized procedures for collecting

POEs on a timely, cost-effective basis, translating the information so that it is understandable to designers and their clients, and getting the information into the design cycle at a point where it is useful. Until recently, user needs analysis (described in Chapter 6) and POE tended to be completely separate activities. Someone would do a needs analysis as part of programming a project. A few years later, after the building was finished and occupied, someone else would come upon the scene to conduct a POE. Now there is a coming together of needs analysis and POE as projects whose design made use of user consultation are being evaluated following occupancy. A good illustration of this coming together is the Michigan mini-park on which Rachel Kaplan consulted prior to development and which she later evaluated.[8]

Evaluation would also be more likely if the designer spent more time in the project following completion. The salutary effects of having the designer physically present in Village Homes and Sea Ranch, two innovative housing developments, has been mentioned. In each case, the designers participated in the ongoing evaluation and fine tuning of the project. The Corbetts used interviews and questionnaires in their evaluation of Village Homes while Halprin relied primarily on workshops for designers and residents.

POE can be used to determine whether the design resulting from a needs analysis has been successful. Interior designer Walter Kleeman and his students made a detailed needs analysis of the Chicago-Reed Mental Health Center.[9] Many of their recommendations were included in the renovation plan. A subsequent evaluation showed that alterations had been successful in improving attitudes towards the building and in raising employee morale. Such surveys should be even more useful in renovation projects whose goal is to improve an existing structure than in new construction, where occupants may not exist in a real sense. It is easier for most people to tell what they like or dislike about their present quarters than for them to predict how they would like something they have not yet experienced.

POE can be distinguished from research in that: (1) it tends to focus on a single type of building, (2) the investigator describes rather than manipulates or changes a setting, (3) the work is almost always conducted under natural conditions rather than in a laboratory, and (4) the major goal of the study is application of the results to improve the same or similar settings.[10] Psychologists who followed a research model in conducting a POE often used procedures that were too time-consuming and expensive. They also were loath to discuss value issues which they considered outside their purview. Resistance to POE also came from designers who were distrustful of lay opinions about their work and from clients who felt that identifying problems would increase occupant dissatisfaction or reflect poorly on past decisions. These concerns were valid to a degree. Used insensitively, POE could legitimize uninformed opinions about buildings. There was little point in asking occupants to comment on mechanical or structural features about which they knew little. In research to develop new products, there is a distinction made between expert panels and market surveys. Both approaches contribute useful information, even though there may be little overlap between them. Expert opinion is the major criterion in design awards within the profession and is the basis of architectural criticism. Such judgments play a valuable role in maintaining and raising professional standards. They do not replace consumer acceptance, which can best be measured by asking the occupants themselves. Under the present system of rewards, there remains the question of how a conscientious designer who attempts to satisfy occupant needs can attract clients. The key to obtaining clients is recognition. Architect Michael Graves put it this way, "If you don't get noticed, you don't get hired."[11] Formal methods of building evaluation may provide opportunities for the architect responsive to occupant needs to gain recognition.

An interesting parallel to the attitudes of some intuitive architects to POE is found in the response of a Native American painter toward the excavation of archeological sites on her tribal grounds. "I had really been opposed to anthropologists and archeologists," artist Kathleen Smith declared. "My idea was that these people dig up our graves."[12] Eventually she decided to join the project in the hopes of obtaining information about her ancestors. She feared that if academics obtained the information and published it in their journals, it would not be accessible to native people. Many architects look upon POE as a type of excavation by outsiders who can only relate to a building on an intellectual level and who are therefore likely to miss what is important. I would suggest to such individuals that they, like Kathleen Smith, join in evaluating buildings to ensure that the questions asked have some architectural relevance. Surveys conducted by psychologists are not likely to include questions about scale, proportion, or other items of primary interest to architects unless architects demand that such issues be considered.

HANDLING CONSUMER COMPLAINTS

Building owners may also resist POE because of the fear that problems that cannot be resolved will be identified and that this will increase occupant frustration. This is a legitimate concern that can be dealt with best by the evaluation team's pointing out to the occupants that a survey isn't going to solve problems by itself. It is only a step on the way toward identifying trouble spots and determining that further action will be needed to correct deficiencies. Identifying sources of consumer dissatisfaction should be seen in a positive light. Such complaints provide useful information for correcting defects in present and future projects. It is much better to identify and deal with problems directly than to leave the consumer angry.

Under pressure from consumer organizations, industry has created consumer relations departments intended to generate good will and provide for some kind of consumer input that would be helpful in monitoring ongoing activities and in developing new products. There is evidence that the development of appropriate procedures for handling consumer complaints can be beneficial to industry. The return is seen in retention of existing customers, reduced regulatory costs, and fewer lawsuits. Effective complaint-handling procedures can detect problems before they become widespread and identify where improvements or new products are needed.[13] A study of ten well-managed companies reported that the majority of new product ideas came from customers.[14] Some major corporations, including IBM and Digital Equipment Corporation, require top managers to spend several weeks a year with customers.[15] Other benefits of adequate complaint-handling procedures are a lessened need for late design changes, an improved image for the company, better relations with the government, and broadened loyalty to the product line. Although the Coca-Cola company receives very few customer complaints, the ones received are taken seriously. A mail survey of customers making complaints found that:

- Customers who felt their complaints had not been satisfactorily resolved told a median of nine to ten people about their negative experiences.
- Customers who were completely satisfied with the response from the company told a median of four to five people about their positive experiences.

Satisfaction with the response from the company determined future patronage. Many of those who felt satisfied with the company's answer increased their consumption of Coca-Cola products, while those who felt their questions had not been answered to their satisfaction no longer buy the products or buy them less often.[16] The nature of design practice, with many "captive occupants" who cannot vote with their feet or their dollars, makes it more difficult to demonstrate the value of good consumer relations than it is in regard to hair lotion or soft drinks, but the same general principle enunciated by Adam Smith, that the satisfaction of consumer needs is the primary justification of the economic system, applies.

SURVEY QUESTIONS

Designers, clients, and occupants should participate in the development of the survey questions. Going uninvited into a building and conducting an evaluation is a sure prescription for having the results ignored. I can offer two contrasting examples from our current studies of consumer cooperatives. In one city we invited ourselves in and conducted member surveys at five stores. We summarized the results for the general manager and for the newsletter and offered to come in and discuss the results further. End of story. I have no indication that the results were ever used.

A happier example is the request that came from a second cooperative to design a survey instrument that they could administer themselves. Barbara Sommer and I spent an afternoon with them composing the questions. A month later we chanced upon a member of the board who told us how useful the results had been. As a result of the survey, the co-op had altered its merchandising policies and made important decisions about expansion. At subsequent board meetings there was frequent mention of the results. Because the survey was planned and carried out by the group themselves rather than by an outside agency, the questions could not be dismissed as irrelevant or the sample as unrepresentative. The same principle applies to POE. Potential users of the information who are involved in a survey from the outset will be more interested in the report and in implementing the findings.

Evaluation is more than a list of weaknesses and problems. The root of the word is value, and this means the good as well as the bad. It is diplomatic to begin a report with compliments rather than criticisms. No matter how inadequate a building, there is always something good that can be said about it. Having identified both strengths and weaknesses, it will be necessary to rank suggested changes in terms of importance and priority. The number of people complaining about an item will not automatically reflect the intensity of their complaints. It may be more important to remedy a defect that is of serious concern to 10 percent of the occupants than to deal with a minor need that everyone recognizes. One approach is to use a combination of rating and ranking procedures. People are asked first to indicate degrees of satisfaction with various architectural elements. After they have gone through the list, they are asked to star or number the top three problems. Another is to begin the survey with a general, open-ended question before using a checklist. The occupant is asked first, "In your own words, what do you like most about the building?" This kind of open-ended format avoids suggesting problems to the respondent.

It is also necessary to wait for the respondent to formulate an answer. Waiting is not easy for someone in a hurry. Sometimes I use a classroom demonstration of how long a minute can last. I ask my students a specific question and then delay a full 60 seconds before allowing anyone to answer. In the leaden silence that follows, a minute is a small eternity. Patience is necessary because occupants have had little previous experience in describing buildings.

The chief impediment to POE today is not a lack of trained people or methods, but the cost in time, effort, and dollars. A typical response to the question, "Wouldn't it be worthwhile to go back in a year's time and take a look at how the building works?" is a terse, "Sorry, it isn't in the budget." In a study of 265 evaluations of housing projects, Bechtel and Srivastavi found that 92 percent had outside funding, and of these the federal government was the largest sponsor, representing 42 percent of all projects, probably more in actual dollars. The dependence of large-scale POE upon outside funding is evident.[17] However, with the tightening of federal funds, it may be necessary for investigators to depend upon local support in the future. Ideally an architectural office could negotiate POE as part of the original contract, with some funds reserved for redesign and change based on the results of the evaluation. To ensure that smaller studies contribute to a larger body of knowledge, some sharing of instruments and approaches will be desirable. There is no need for each investigator to reinvent the wheel and develop a new instrument that does not allow comparison with the results of previous studies. Some combination of general questions useful in most buildings of a given type and questions specific to the setting can be used.

There has been sporadic interest in mandating POE for major governmental construction. In 1980 Senate Bill 2080, requiring post-occupancy evaluation, was passed by the U.S. Senate but was never voted out of committee in the House. I feel it is premature to attempt such a massive program at this time. I would recommend trying out this approach on a small scale, perhaps involving one or two building types in one agency, before it becomes a requirement for all projects. Such exploratory use would demonstrate where evaluation makes a difference and where it would be unproductive. Like others who have advocated systematic evaluation of social programs, I have been sadly disappointed at how this has worked in practice, where "evaluation" became mere records-keeping, or else massive experimental studies whose results came far too late to be useful.

Lon Wheeler used an interesting construction-evaluation-redesign model in Terre Haute, Indiana.[18] Wheeler's firm was hired to build a series of college dormitories. They built the first one, evaluated it to determine the changes that were necessary, and incorporated these improvements into the second building. Then they evaluated the second dormitory and included the improvements needed into the design of the third building. Although a federal mandate for POE on all government buildings would provide a quick fix of dollars, I think the long-term effects would be less satisfactory than a gradual approach attempting to learn where POE can make a difference.

When used properly and sensitively, POE can give a firm a competitive edge in obtaining new work and retaining clients. When I was part of a panel convened to select architects for a major prison construction contract, we interviewed firms with extensive experience in the field. One firm had designed 70 prisons and jails with a total capacity of 25,000 beds and a dollar value of $1.3 billion. This was topped by another firm that had completed 75 correctional institutions. A single architect with another team had personally directed more than 60 detention projects. What was lacking in these presentations *without exception* was evidence of how well the buildings worked. There were no data presented to indicate whether these were good jails or poor jails. We were shown slides, but they were carefully selected, and were mostly exterior views from unusual angles or interior shots taken before the building opened.

Some of these firms interested in the jail project had spent thousands of dollars in responding to the request for a proposal. They had prepared expensive brochures and scale models, and had brought in outside experts to strengthen their cases. One team flew in two prison wardens and an outside consultant from across the continent to give ten-minute presentations. All this was undertaken without any promise of payment. Technically, the firm selected for the project could not receive any direct reimbursement for the expenses contracted in preparing the proposal. In relation to these unremunerated front-end expenses, the cost of 200 hours of employee time to conduct a POE at the end of a project does not seem so significant. While there appears to be a stronger financial incentive for a firm to write a proposal than to do a POE, there is a connection between POEs on past projects and subsequent proposals. Our selection panel would have been responsive to solid information that an earlier facility designed by a firm had been successful. This could have been presented as data on breakage, vandalism, escapes, repair and maintenance costs, temperature range, and energy use, as well as intangible measures involving the responses of guards, administrators, inmates, and townspeople. It would be economically feasible for a firm to obtain some of this information, and even a small amount at least demonstrates a firm's continuing interest in its buildings.

In conducting a POE, physical measurements should be taken in actuality rather than copied from building specifications. Changes occur because of renovations, breakdowns, and the practices of the occupants. The ventilation may be satisfactory on paper, but when partitions are introduced, circulation patterns are altered so that some areas are excessively breezy and others stuffy. Illumination levels at a county jail I visited were excellent in the building's specifications, but the inmates had placed brown paper bags over most of the lights so that they could watch television during the day because there was nothing else to do. As a result, illumination was too low for reading or writing letters.

PUBLISHING EVALUATIONAL STUDIES

Presently there is no standard format for presenting POEs. As more POEs are done and people start comparing buildings, a common format is likely to emerge. This will in turn encourage the use of standardized instruments and lists of criteria that apply to a variety of building types. Gordon Allport differentiated between ideographic and nomothetic approaches in science.[19] Ideographic investigations are detailed case studies of individual events emphasizing their uniqueness. Nomothetic studies are group comparisons that emphasize the commonalities among those items in a category. Allport believed that both types of investigations are necessary. While psychology has gone the route of the physical sciences in emphasizing group comparisons (nomothetic studies) and downplaying case studies, architectural research has tended to emphasize the ideographic approach to buildings, neighborhoods, and communities. The danger of the case study is that too much attention is paid to the particular and not enough to the general. There also seems to be an unfortunate bias in case studies to concentrate on the negative and ignore the positive.

The major considerations in writing a POE are how much detail and what aspects of a building will interest the client. One could write anything from a paragraph to an entire volume about a building. If I went through my home examining every feature with a serious eye, I could come up with a monograph. I could also describe my house in a single paragraph. There aren't any ground rules for a writer of a POE governing breadth or depth of coverage. This variability and spottiness reduces the potential value of the technique for influencing practice. It is unreasonable to expect a busy designer to wade through a hundred-page monograph in the hopes of finding a few snippets of useful information, or, on the other hand, to be satisfied with incomplete information.

Another issue in publishing evaluational studies concerns the proper outlet for them. Design journals cannot afford to devote much space to evaluational studies, considering the range of building types in existence and the detail necessary to be useful to practitioners. However there is a difference between publishing a full-scale study and including evaluational information in a report on a specific project. I strongly believe that building descriptions in architectural journals *must* contain evaluational data. It is irrational to see pictures and read descriptions of buildings without knowing how they work for the occupants. It is like hearing about a wonderful design for a new boat without knowing whether the boat will float. The evaluational section does not have to be long and detailed. An article about an office building, for example, might state that interviews were conducted with 15 managerial and 15 clerical employees and 40 visitors to the building. The highest level of satisfaction was expressed toward ________, and the least satisfaction expressed toward ________, and the people felt that improvements were most needed in the area of ________ and ________.

The logical outlet for a POE would be a periodical concerned with the building type being discussed. The evaluation of an office building might be in a periodical magazine concerned with offices. From a bibliography on open-plan offices compiled in 1977 by Paoletti and Lewitz Associates, an acoustical consulting firm in San Francisco, the list of periodicals that have published articles on offices includes *The Office, Modern Office Procedures, Administrative Office Management, Management World, International Management, Contract Magazine, Plant Engineering, Building Research and Practice, Building Science,* and *Skyscraper Management.*

Despite the great proliferation of topical magazines, most environmental researchers are unfamiliar with them because they are not available in university or research libraries. Many are proprietary journals and some only publish articles by their own writers. A reference librarian can be extraordinarily helpful in locating the appropriate outlet. When I began to study airports, I had no idea where the findings could be published. The reference librarian came up with *Air Travel World,* a periodical that I had never seen before and have not seen since. Later we did a study of a veterinary hospital. The results did not have sufficient generality or theoretical significance to interest designers or social scientists. The only group likely to be interested in the results would be veterinarians. Our search for a possible outlet came up with the *California Veterinarian,* which eagerly published the evaluation and requested additional articles from us.

Approached in the right way, a farsighted publisher of trade periodicals might be willing to devote a section to building evaluations. At least there might be a section listing POEs along with names and addresses of people who can supply additional information. Such periodicals will not be read by designers or social scientists but by people with job titles like "Facilities Manager" or "Space Planner" who have direct access to decision-makers. They may at some future time call an article to the attention of the designer working with the firm on a particular project. In this way the evaluation published in a topical journal will be used to improve design practice. I do not want to create the impression that publishing in trade journals is without problems. As a rule these magazines will not publish articles that might offend advertisers. Profit-oriented periodicals feel little obligation to present all views on a subject. In spite of these difficulties, I feel that it is essential for environmental researchers to publish POEs in places where they will be read by people who design, manage, and occupy the buildings that are the subjects of the evaluations.

WHO WILL FOOT THE BILL?

The benefits from social design accrue most readily to the occupants, both present and future, and to the client. The architect will not be eager to hire someone who might decide that a new building isn't necessary or to find out how a building worked out after it was completed. Architectural contracts are not written to support post-occupancy evaluation. There is money for prior planning but not for follow-up work. Few clients are willing to pay their architect to evaluate their building and identify problems so that the architect, on the next job, can design a better building, possibly for a competitor. The only place a client conceivably would pay for a POE is at the beginning of the process, where lessons learned would contribute directly to a better building for them. The problem is that Company B is not going to let Company A's architects evaluate their buildings, discover its problems, and then build a better building for

Company A. There is some hope for this model in large companies or government departments that are constructing a succession of buildings of the same general type where knowledge learned would directly benefit the client organization.

Most of the involvement of social scientists in the design process was funded by government agencies or some third party and not by architectural offices. The ideal situation would have been for the needs analysis or POE to be supported by a consumer organization. Unfortunately, tenants are unorganized and unable to fund studies of buildings. I have never heard of a tenants' organization hiring an environmental psychologist to conduct a post-occupancy evaluation. I have been asked to evaluate prison conditions as part of inmate class action lawsuits, but the request came from the public defender, not the inmates. Frank Becker evaluated numerous public housing projects in New York State, but his client was a state agency rather than a tenants' organization, although the tenants were the chief beneficiaries of his study.[20]

At least for the time being, it seems as if these activities must be supported by third parties. This places social design in the same category as medical research or advanced scholarship in the humanities. Most medical research is supported by universities as part of their general mission to advance knowledge, or by the federal government in an effort to prevent and cure disease, or by drug companies that hope to find new uses for their products. Support for research in the humanities and social sciences is even more clearly identified with the federal government, private foundations, and universities. Such examples make clear that there are many worthy activities that are not supported either by practitioners or by consumers of the service.

It is also possible to view POE as a responsibility of the designer. This would provide an economic base, but at some cost in objectivity. It is difficult to see how a valid information bank on buildings could result from studies supported by practicing architects. Only a third party, such as a professional society, government agency, or a university department would be capable of supporting truly objective studies. A design bank for convalescent hospitals might be compiled and supported by the American Gerontological Society, the Department of Health and Human Services, or by a particular architecture school. I believe that there is merit in the model described in *Design Awareness*, in which each design school would collect information about a single building type and make it available to others through an information network.[21] I am aware of only one instance during the past decade of this model's being implemented—the National Clearinghouse for Criminal Justice Architecture and Planning in Urbana, Illinois, whose director was a faculty member in the University Department of Architecture. Supported by a branch of the U.S. Department of Justice, the Clearinghouse collected state-of-the-art information about prisons and jails and evaluated plans for new construction.

Other groups that cross professional lines and serve some of these same purposes have operated on a less formal basis. In 1976 the Wilderness Psychology Group was founded to remedy what was seen as the preoccupation of environmental researchers with the urban environment. Four years later, the group was a multi-disciplinary network of almost 100 individuals from psychology, geography, forestry, and recreation. Another interest group has been formed around the topic of pedestrian behavior. They publish a newsletter and hold panel discussions at various professional meetings on the design and use of streets, sidewalks, plazas, and other pedestrian areas. Within the division of Population and Environmental Psychology of the American Psychological Association, there is an informal network of psychologists interested in energy issues who hold occasional meetings and share unpublished materials. These newsletters and meetings do not constitute an open-ended design information service, but they accomplish some of the same purposes in compilation and dissemination.

Design schools have available the enthusiasm and talent of their students and faculties, which makes the collection of information feasible at a modest cost. What I like most about such a program is that it is a decentralized enterprise. Each school or department would choose a particular building type and then develop appropriate categories and tools for compiling and disseminating the information. I have seen this system work successfully on a local level. The city in which I live became the nexus for disseminating information about municipal energy conservation. Eventually the major private utility in the state contributed $23,000 to support an energy conservation coordinator to answer queries from around the world. About half the inquiries come from professionals such as city planners, architects, and members of private governmental bodies. The city also sells publications describing its energy policies and the proceeds help support the dissemination activities. Prices range from $2 for a copy of the Davis Energy Conservation Building Ordinance to $75 for the Environmental Impact Report on the general plan. It does not seem unreasonable that an architecture department could become the state-of-the-art repository of information on particular building types or techniques, such as cold weather construction, passive solar, and so on.

Some specialization among the various design programs is

already occurring. This stems from the need to focus on a specific setting in order to know previous work and to meet the needs of funding agencies. Architectural programs at the University of Michigan and the University of Southern California have emphasized the study of environments for the elderly. For many years the University of Illinois School of Architecture has investigated buildings and facilities for the physically disabled. The Environmental Psychology program at City University of New York has a longstanding interest in, among other issues, urban parks and neighborhood open spaces. It would not be too much of a jump to go beyond this research interest to the systematic collection of evaluations of completed projects in this specialty area and then on to their dissemination. Some type of seed money would probably be necessary to get this program in operation.

The examples of POEs that follow were deliberately chosen to represent varying degrees of comprehensiveness and expense. The library evaluation was done by an architecture student in several months time with a total budget of under $1,000, while the prison study was carried out by a team of investigators over three years with an $80,000 grant from the British Home Office. Both small-scale and large-scale evaluations have their place in design research.

EXAMPLES

A. Public Library Branches

An architecture firm hired to prepare a renovation plan for the public library system in Berkeley, California, brought in architecture student Michael Durkin to conduct a POE.[22] A modest amount of money was allocated for this purpose (under $1,000) and the study had to be done speedily. Two of the city's libraries had been constructed in the early 1920s and the third in the 1960s. If the study had taken place on a larger scale, for example, a statewide assessment of libraries, some sampling would have been necessary to select representative buildings.

Durkin visited each site to get some feeling for the neighborhoods, the buildings, the users, and the activities taking place. It can be risky to assume one knows in advance exactly how a building is used and by whom. Durkin also read available materials on library layout and usage. On the basis of the visits and previous studies, Durkin constructed survey instruments for library staff and patrons. Had more time and funds been available, it would have been useful to interview nonusers of the library, as was done in the survey by the architectural firm of Deasy, Bolling, and Gill for the Los Angeles public library system.[23] The survey forms were deliberately made brief in order to obtain a good sampling of library patrons.

Most readers were willing to participate in a five- to ten-minute survey. The low refusal rate (only two people out of 236 approached) confirmed the value of using the brief questionnaires, which were given out randomly to groups of people in the library at the time of Durkin's visit. People were approached in various parts of the library with the request that they fill out a questionnaire and leave it in a collection box at the circulation desk. The importance of quiet in libraries dictated the use of written instruments rather than oral interviews. There are other settings, such as public parks or plazas, where interviews would have been more appropriate since people are on the move, writing is difficult, and conversation will not bother people.

SURVEY FORMS

1A. Library Use Indicator. This questionnaire (Figure 17) was designed to pinpoint the most prevalent activities at each branch. It contained a list of 11 activities that people commonly do in the library, and space to write in additional items. While it may seem obvious that the library is used for reading, this is not always the case. Some people come to find reference materials while others want to listen to records. City libraries are also places where students come to study after school and lonely people congregate. Each respondent was also asked how often he or she came to this branch of the library or to other library branches.

FIGURE 17 Activity survey of library patrons.

Date ____________
Time ____________
Library ____________
Age ____________

This questionnaire was designed to discover what people use the library for. Please check any element on the list which applies to you.

________ Check out a book
________ Browse
________ Study
________ Read a newspaper
________ Read a magazine
________ Find specific information about something
________ Relax
________ Meet with friends
________ Make new friends

Continued

FIGURE 17 (Continued)

_______ Do research for school or job
_______ Do work but don't use library material
_______ Other (please specify)

How frequently do you come to this branch of the Berkeley Library System?

Do you use any other branches of the Berkeley Library System, including the Main Library? _______ If so, which ones and why?

What role do you feel this branch of the Berkeley Library System should play in the Berkeley community?

Additional Comments: (Use back of page if you need more space).

Thank you for your cooperation. Please leave the questionnaire in the designated box at the exit when you leave.

1B. General Environment. Each person was asked to rate 28 aspects of the environment (for example, lighting, table arrangement, and privacy) along three-point scales—good, OK, or poor. When an item was rated as deficient, the respondent was asked the reason. Space was left for additional comments.

1C. Distractions. Earlier studies had found that library patrons were reluctant to criticize aspects of a building they greatly valued. Thus it was necessary to develop a questionnaire specifically focused on negative factors. From a list of 14 possible distractions, respondents were asked to check those that annoyed them at that particular time. Additional comments on deficiencies were solicited.

1D. Connotations. This rating scale was used to investigate subjective response to the building and consisted of 30 pairs of polar adjectives (friendly-unfriendly, dark-light, exciting-boring) which were separated by five-point scales.

The final sample consisted of 234 patrons and 24 staff members at the three libraries. Patrons each filled out one of the four forms, staff members filled out 1B, 1C, and 1D. The results were hand-tabulated and summarized in a report for the architectural office that was later distributed to the library staff. The use of a computer would have permitted a more sophisticated analysis of the results, but there was not sufficient money available for this purpose. The economics of the project determined the types of instruments that would be used (brief written survey forms), sample size, and the methods of analyzing and reporting the results.

B. Jails and Prisons

A more extensive POE is the report on penal institutions prepared by David Canter under contract with the British Home Office.[24] The initial discussions for the study took place over a three-year period with a committee of 12 people representing the various Home Office interests, including present and former wardens, architectural consultants, and the like. Once the study was formally begun, the work of collecting and analyzing the information and preparing the final report took another three years. The project was divided into three phases overlapping in time. Phase One involved tours of 16 prisons and interviews with the chief administrator or deputy. Phase Two involved observation of routines and interviews with staff and inmates. Based on the information gathered, separate questionnaires for inmates (Figure 18) and staff were developed. During Phase Three, the questionnaires were administered in six prisons that represented the major categories of penal institutions.

Additional procedures were used to obtain information. Records were examined, including the architect's drawings and prison reports. There was a physical inspection of various parts of each facility to check whether areas were being used as listed on the plans. A recreation yard may be closed off because of a lack of staff or a shop may be converted into a dormitory due to crowding. The evaluation team looked for "physical traces" of occupancy, including chair arrangements, the condition of equipment, the general level of cleanliness, and the condition of the grounds areas. Official records were perused to determine daily occupancy rate, inmate age, and duration of sentence. Like the architect's drawings, such information will not be perfectly accurate or current, but it is relevant and necessary.

Interviews were conducted with inmates and with all levels of staff. The generally high level of distrust in prisons made it unfeasible to tape record sessions. Brief notes were taken of the respondents' answers and these were elaborated by the researcher afterwards. Two discussion sessions with inmates were held in one of the institutions, the first to discuss the existing facility and the second to plan a reorganization of the interior layout.

An observer toured each building at various times of the day to record space usage. The evaluation team also improvised techniques that were especially suited to a penal setting. One of these

UNIVERSITY OF SURREY
PRISON DESIGN AND USE STUDY
(Confidential)

This questionnaire is part of a study of prison and borstal buildings as seen by those who live and work in them.

By asking those who know these places best we expect to obtain an accurate picture of their experience of conditions in these institutions.

To preserve the anonymous nature of the information PLEASE DO NOT WRITE your name on this questionnaire.

You may write in pencil or biro.

When completed, place your questionnaire in the sealed collection box marked "University of Surrey".

For office use only

Establishment .... ☐1

Wing or House .... ☐2

Floor (tick) Ground ☐ 1st ☐ ☐3

Please tick the boxes which apply to you:

Remand ☐ Sentenced ☐ ☐4 ☐7

Red Band ☐

Rule 43 ☐

Time spent in this establishment Years .... Months .... Weeks .... ☐8 ☐9 ☐10

Your accommodation:

Single cubicle ☐

Single cell ☐

Doubled-up cell ☐

Tripled-up cell ☐ ☐12 ☐13

Shared room ☐ How many people share? ☐

Usual workplace (if any) .... ☐14

Please answer the following questions by circling one number
If you are unfamiliar with any place referred to in a question, leave the answer blank.

LAYOUT OF THE ESTABLISHMENT

	very easy	generally easy	fairly easy	neither easy nor difficult	fairly difficult	generally difficult	very difficult	
On arriving at this establishment how easy was it for you to get to know the layout of the buildings in relation to one another?	1	2	3	4	5	6	7	☐15
Does the position of the Probation office affect the ease or difficulty of meeting probation staff?	1	2	3	4	5	6	7	☐19
Does the layout of the establishment make it difficult or easy for you to meet inmates from other accommodation areas? (tick if not applicable) ☐	1	2	3	4	5	6	7	☐20

	very satisfactory	generally satisfactory	fairly satisfactory	neither satisfactory nor unsatisfactory	fairly unsatisfactory	generally unsatisfactory	very unsatisfactory	
How satisfactory or unsatisfactory is the position of the kitchen for distributing meals to inmates?	1	2	3	4	5	6	7	☐22
How satisfactory or unsatisfactory is the location of the Wing Manager's office for contact with inmates?	1	2	3	4	5	6	7	☐23

FIGURE 18 First page of prison inmate survey.

was a card-sorting procedure in which both inmates and staff were asked to classify various types of institutions and areas within the prison in terms of similarities or differences between them. The purpose was to identify those areas and institutions that seemed to fill roughly the same functions.

Written questionnaires were collected from staff and inmates in six institutions. This part of the study was not without its problems, including the illiteracy of some inmates as well as difficulty in obtaining cooperation and assuring the confidentiality of the replies. Some prison staff were reluctant to allow inmate questionnaires to leave the institution uncensored. The research team had agreed that an official should have access to the questionnaires in every institution. Such compromises with proper scientific methodology are unfortunate, but they cannot always be avoided. In this particular project it appeared that little or no censorship of the inmate replies occurred. The questionnaires were constructed so as to facilitate computer scoring. A report summarizing the findings was delivered to the Home Office after the study was completed.

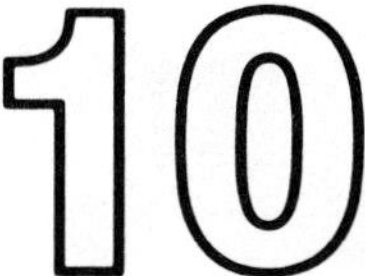

COMMUNITY ARTS PROGRAMS

In writing about architecture, it is important not to neglect art. The art world of the 1960s was subjected to the same types of pressures that produced social design in architecture. There was a crisis of purpose and communication among artists, and between them and the public. Artists were painting for one another and for a narrow circle of collectors, gallery owners, and critics. New styles burst on the scene to satisfy the novelty hunger of the media. Exhibits became more outrageous as the pressures for public exposure became more frantic. The potential of art for enriching people's lives was lost in the quest for instant fame and dollars.

Abstract expressionism accurately reflected the turmoil of the times, in which artists saw as their role the deliberate violation of middle-class standards. The underclass of America did not figure in this game of insulting the middle class to amuse the wealthy. Art critics supported this attitude by ignoring and downgrading audience response. If untrained people did not like the work, perhaps this was the wrong audience for it or the wrong location for the exhibit. The result was an art sealed off from a general audience, which excluded anyone who was not a professional artist, critic, gallery owner, or collector.

Albert Camus advocated art that was not so weighted down with leaden boots that it could not soar to heights of imagination, nor should it be so loose and free from reality that it would drift with every breeze.[1] The art world of the mid-1960s was in danger of blowing away. Its practitioners either rejected meaning entirely in the search for ultimate self-expression, or treated it with ridicule. There were also problems of public access. If a sculptor created work that could enrich people's lives, it was doubtful that many of its potential audience would see it, hidden away in private galleries or executive suites. Problems of access were most acute for those artists whose work was not favored by the establishment, for example, women whose impressive work in fabric, ceramics, and portraiture was dismissed as mere craft, and minority artists who saw little in the professional schools and exhibits that meant anything to their people.

This situation laid the basis for a new type of art intended to strengthen people's connections to their surroundings and to deeper themes of human existence. The artist's role changed from producing artwork for well-to-do collectors to creating art in public locations with the help of neighborhood residents. To fulfill this new role, artists learned how to solicit building owners, city officials, local merchants, and government agencies for funds, materials, and equipment. The public shifted from being passive spectators to active participants in the work, and a community art movement was born.

RELATION TO SOCIAL DESIGN

The new art was related to social design in its origins in the civil rights and environmental movements, its site in the community, its goal of increasing people's connections to their surroundings, and in its reliance on consultation and participation. The concern with civil rights was expressed in themes of cultural history and universal justice, and in the attempt to bring art to the poor. The environmental connection was the goal of brightening urban spaces and at the same time increasing people's awareness of their surroundings. Just as social design brought architects and planners out of their studios to talk with potential occupants and encouraged behavioral scientists to leave the laboratory to observe behavior in the real world, community art encouraged painters to leave their studios, not in search of a wider canvas on which ego could be displayed, but to seek out inspiration and purpose in the life of the community and to bring art to the neighborhoods. There were common problems of funding and introducing participatory methods to people who had previously been excluded from decisions. Painters trained in an individualistic mode experienced the same difficulty in shifting to a cooperative format that young architects trained to design *for* people had in designing *with* people. In each case the journey to participatory methods was not an easy one because there were so few signposts, markers, or maps.

Many programs of neighborhood rehabilitation included both building renovation according to social design principles and public art with community consultation. Where a garden plot or mini-park had been created by local residents, a community mural was likely to be nearby. When school officials and parent groups in San Francisco attempted to humanize the prison-like school yards, they embarked on simultaneous programs of building renovation and art. Students, parents, teachers, and custodians joined to create mosaics, sculpture, stained glass, and murals. They obtained picks and jackhammers to remove asphalt so that trees and flowers could be planted. At the Estrada Courts Housing Project in Los Angeles, murals were the chosen method for upgrading the dismal buildings and the concrete-block wall surrounding the project. Largely out of a concern for decreasing the incidence of vandalism, city officials enthusiastically supported the idea. What occurred next was not hiring professional artists to come in and drop off their sculpture or decorate the walls and then leave, but bringing in artists to assist local residents create artwork. The mural has been a favored device in community arts programs. Its large scale encourages cooperation and community input. Of all types of painting, wall art is closest to architecture since it is generally inseparable from the site. More than 100 murals were completed at Estrada Courts, which became a showplace of mural art. Visitors have come from all over the globe to see the work, and this attention has been a source of great pride to residents, especially to those who participated in the painting. When I last visited the project, not a single one of the murals had been touched by graffiti, yet virtually all the surrounding walls had been hit. It seemed clear that people respected art that respected their lives.[2]

Murals for the Neighborhoods

Following a series of riots that devastated many portions of Detroit's black neighborhoods, community leaders decided that something had to be done to increase neighborhood pride. The elders at one church contracted artist Jim Malone, who asked his colleagues to submit sketches of famous black people that Malone then assembled into a Wall of Pride. The Chicago mural movement had begun in 1967 with the Wall of Respect, directed by William Walker. Portraying the lives of famous black people, it was supported by the Organization of Black Artists of Chicago and the 43rd Street Organization. Walls with similar themes of black history have appeared in Atlanta, St. Louis, New York, and other American cities. Celebration of cultural history was one of the many deeply conservative themes depicted in community art. In the Hispanic barrios, the most common mural themes were the family and *La Raza*. Under sponsorship of the Los Angeles Mural Program, professional artists worked with street gangs in selecting locations, designing, and painting walls. In New York City, a wall painting 100 feet long and 50 feet high titled "Arise from Oppression" was coordinated by artist Jim Januzzi under the auspices of the Cityarts Workshop and was designed by 25 Puerto Rican youths. Almost 200 people joined in the actual painting over a period of several months.

An earlier mural renaissance in the United States occurred

during the Great Depression, when unemployed artists were hired under the Works Projects Administration (WPA) to decorate public buildings. Over 3600 artists participated in this program and more than 16,000 works in various media were produced. An interesting innovation on many projects was the removal of artists' names from their submissions. Mural designs and sculpture models were submitted unsigned. The name of the entrant was not disclosed until after the award was made.[3]

Following the Second World War a number of municipalities and states passed "percentage for art" regulations that required that a certain percentage of the budget for civic construction be used for art. These programs began in the late 1950s in Philadelphia and Baltimore as part of urban rehabilitation. By 1982 more than 65 state and local governments had such programs in operation.[4] Further assistance came from two federal agencies. The General Services Administration initiated its Art-in-Architecture project in 1962, and the National Endowment for the Arts started a program in 1967 for Art in Public Places. These are being continued even in times of shrinking government budgets. It is noteworthy that the previous mural explosion in the United States occurred during the Great Depression. The association between public art and concern with poverty may be more than coincidental.[5]

The community art of the 1960s differed from its predecessors in several respects. Most of the WPA murals were done indoors and little effort was made to involve neighborhood people. It was a matter of professionals bringing art into places where people would see it. In the community arts of the 1960s, artists worked with local people to produce art for outdoor locations, and neighborhood people were involved at every stage of the operation. The projects were frequently supported by funds available under the Comprehensive Employment and Training Act (CETA), intended to provide job training for the unemployed. There were CETA-sponsored dance, theater, and visual arts programs.

The amount of consultation and public participation on mural projects varied from one city to the next. The first task of the community artist was to raise awareness. Often this meant that a muralist started work alone. Once the painting was in process, people would stop to ask questions and find out what was happening. They hesitantly assisted in mixing the paints, priming the walls, and finally, with more confidence in their abilities, joining in the actual painting. The preliminaries broke down barriers and created interest. James Marson Fitch maintained that physical proximity between artist and audience stimulated both—the one to more intense creativity, the other to a heightened response.[6] Art in public makes the line of communication between artist and audience short and incandescent. Community murals are a source of pride not simply because they are located in a neighborhood but because they were planned with and often painted by local residents.

Community artists do not view their work as mere decoration of architecture. Many of the buildings on which the murals were painted were slated for demolition or rehabilitation. The selection of neglected walls for painting has changed somewhat with the advent of the "percentage for art" programs. This has provided some community artists with access to walls on major public buildings. Not all architects welcome mural art. Some view it as a distraction from the building. Moshe Safdie considers it an unnecessary adornment:

> *When I was doing Habitat, I was bombarded by painters and sculptors who wanted the opportunity to do a mural here, a sculpture there. At first I just avoided them without really knowing why. And then I realized that most often when so-called fine art was put in architecture, it was like make-up, compensating for the inability of the architecture to respond to life in such a way that it satisfies our emotions. . . . A total and comprehensive design will result in a place that does not need to be saved by art.*[7]

Safdie's statement can be partially explained by the art he was thinking of when he wrote it. In his book, *Beyond Habitat,* he comments that most current painting and sculpture is not significant to him. "I respond more to microphotographs of rock crystals or animal cells than to most of the paintings of today," Safdie observed.[8] I agree that Habitat at this time does not require murals or exterior sculpture. The variegated patterns, strong concrete imagery, and the individual gardens for each apartment make this unnecessary. Yet I am unwilling to accept the view that the only legitimate reason for public art is to fill some omission in the architecture—to attempt to save a flawed building through decoration. Painting and sculpture can have a place in a well-designed project, and that place can be specified in advance during negotiations between artist, owner, and future occupants.

Community art is not studio painting out-of-doors. Many of the murals painted by professional artists under corporate sponsorship involved no consultation with local residents. Nor is it restricted to a particular format. For the area around Grant's Tomb in New York City, the Cityarts program staff involved local youth in designing and laying ceramic tiles and creating sculptural benches. While some formats such as mural painting lend themselves more easily than others to participation, there is no requirement that community art be restricted to murals. Nor is community art merely painting or sculpture with a social message. Sometimes a single artist working alone can create a work that expresses community values. Yet the risk is that without consultation, the message may be that of the artist and not that of the community. Some painters may want to flaunt their political or social ideals on the walls to "spit in the eye" of the community. Jean Charlot, one of the Mexican muralists of the 1920s, declared that his objective was to "ram down the throats of the bourgeoisie the consciousness of defeat and a squirming sense of their social predicament."[9] This may be social art or political art, but it is not community art, whose distinguishing characteristic is consultation between artists and their audience. Without discussion, it does not matter if the work is done out-of-doors or contains a social message; it is not community art.

The issue of political expression is particularly relevant to murals, which often combine words and pictures. The good muralist struggles constantly to preserve meaningful content without becoming a sloganeer. The content of a mural should be clear to its audience. Unlike the studio painter, the community artist cannot count on an art critic to interpret vague symbols. Art critics don't pay much attention to murals and the audience for the mural does not read much art criticism.

The major difference between community and studio art is that the former is site specific. The studio painter does not know how or where a canvas will be displayed. Even if the purchaser is known in advance, the painting may be sold to someone else or moved.[10] The mural painter knows where a work will go and who will be seeing it, and takes into account environmental elements such as available light and shadow, neighborhood life, and building details. The artist escapes from a limited audience to one that will view it in a public location. This does not mean that the artist will be overcome by a desire to paint "down" to local residents, but that the logic will demand the use of symbols that are both simpler and broader in their appeal.[11]

Outdoor murals exposed to wind, sun, rain, and vandalism tend to be impermanent, at least in comparison to studio canvases. The neglected buildings chosen for murals are often soon to be rehabilitated or razed. The typical community mural will not last five years. Some are painted over within a year. Even the best works, where the artist has a firm commitment from the building owner not to remove the painting, and the proper primer, paint, and sealant have been used, will not last more than 30 years. Transience frees the community artist from the obligation of creating timeless

FIGURE 19 Teenage residents of Estrada Courts Housing Project in Los Angeles were hired to paint murals and designs on buildings and the fence around the site.

FIGURE 20 Children, parents, teachers, and the custodians joined to paint murals to counteract the prison-like exterior of this Chicago school.

FIGURE 21 A county arts association painted colorful replicas of U.S. stamps on all four sides of their rural post office.

FIGURE 22 Two murals painted on public toilets were spared by graffitists, although surrounding walls in this neighborhood park were hit.

pieces. It also creates a niche for those who would document mural art. The photograph of a wall painting will outlast the work and even the building on which it has been painted. Documentation was a role that social scientists played in the new mural movement.[12] However, there was not the same coming together of artists and behavioral scientists that had characterized social design. Artists evolved their own techniques of consultation with neighborhood residents. There was very little systematic needs analysis or evaluation of completed works. Perhaps as a result, community art never had the same impact in art schools that social design had in schools of architecture and city planning. It is interesting to speculate whether more significant involvement of behavioral scientists in documentation and evaluation would have resulted in a greater acceptance of community murals within the professional art world. Currently there are very few scheduled courses or programs in mural painting taught at major art schools.

The community artist must be able to work with diverse groups. This is no task for the prima donna who knows what is best for others and doesn't care whether or not they like the work. The ability to accept criticism gracefully is a requirement. There will be some people who like the painting and some who do not. To reconcile the inevitability of controversy with the model of community consultation requires vision, tact, and a great store of patience. In a society where everyone shares the same traditions and values, a representational mural does not have the same potential for conflict that it does in a divided society. One can sympathize with the artist who decides to do an abstract mosaic or a geometric stainless steel design for a downtown plaza. If there is any objection to the lack of form or message, this will probably be less than the controversy that content would bring. Most disputes about content are not *created* by the artist, but they exist in the society and are brought out into the open by the attempt to deal with important issues. The processes of consultation in creating a piece of public art are likely to make the work itself seem bland by comparison.

I attended a workshop conducted by a state arts agency on selecting art for public institutions in which the issue of professional standards dominated the discussion. Adherents of the high-art approach wanted all the works to be selected by a paid jury of professionals in the state capital. Based upon those selections already made by the agency for other settings, the likely result would be abstract sculpture at the entrances to prisons and op-art paintings in the corridors. Community artists wanted the employees and the inmates to have a significant voice in selecting the work. This approach was strongly resisted by the high-art advocates, who doubted that local people would select good art. Giving people what they wanted, they argued, would pander to local tastes and not elevate them as work selected by experts might do. They also expressed the fear that local people would prefer reproductions of Norman Rockwell and Andrew Wyeth to original pieces selected by art experts.

The bringing of abstract sculpture by professional artists into prisons is analogous to performing grand opera there. The work is far beyond the sensibilities and tastes of inmates and staff. While a single performance might be considered a novelty, a weekly grand opera would seem bizarre. A minimalist painting or op-art sculpture that people could not understand and could not avoid because it was located in a central corridor or visiting room would become an object of derision and even hatred. Rather than the inmates' appreciating the amount of money to be spent for art in the institution and thereby elevating their feelings of self-worth, the work would be a continual reminder of their powerlessness and alienation from the larger society and its standards.

The community artist's contribution, like that of the social designer, will be embodied less in a signed plaque or award than in a finished product and the pride of the residents who assisted. Most community murals are unsigned. This is particularly true when a large number of people has been involved. It would be distracting to list 20 names on a mural, destructive of the goals of community art to list only the leaders, and impossible to list the 200 participants involved in the noted "Arise from Oppression" mural in New York City. Professional artists such as Judy Baca, Susan Green, and John Weber, who have been active in community art, do not expect to see their names displayed, nor do they expect awards or prizes. There may be a ceremony at the dedication of the work and a photograph in the newspaper that can be added to a portfolio. The chief sources of satisfaction are in the work itself and the appreciation of the local residents. This relative anonymity parallels that of the social designer who develops a plan by which employees will be able to choose colors for their work areas or who assists housing project residents to draw up a landscape plan for the exterior areas. This calling requires a generous attitude rather than a display of ego.

Community murals are a metaphor of social design in architecture. The worth of a community mural is judged not according to formal criteria of line, proportion, and verisimilitude, but the degree to which it meets the needs of those who must live with it. Like buildings, a mural on a downtown street is inescapable for local residents. While the products of social design and community art are different, the objectives of increased awareness and connection to the environment through participation are similar.

EXAMPLES

A. Procedures in Applying for a Mural

The following guidelines had been prepared by the City-Wide Mural Project, started in 1974 as an adjunct of the Department of Recreation and Parks, City of Los Angeles. Out of the project came the Mural Resource Center, making technical, artistic, and legal information on public art available to community artists and to the interested public. The Mural Resource Center has a slide collection, an art library, legal information on copyrights, and distributes maps of Los Angeles murals.

1. Any community artist who lives in the City of Los Angeles is eligible to propose either a team mural to be done with senior citizens, children or adolescents of her/his community, or an individual mural. We encourage group murals.
2. The artist will be required to present a portfolio of his/her work and sketch for the mural.
3. The artist selects a wall to be painted within her/his community and obtains permission for this wall from the owner, the council, and MRC staff.
4. As there are more applicants in every community than our program can accommodate, we make choices. These decisions are based on artistic merit and relevance to our program.
5. The artist will take the completed sketch to the community and get approval through a signed petition. The community signed petition of the approved mural is turned into the Citywide Mural Project. At that time, the artist will sign a contract with us, receiving $50.00, for the sketch and $345.00, upon completion of the mural, which totals $395.00.
6. We will supply 15 gallons of paint and brushes per mural, and the necessary scaffolding, which you will be responsible for.
7. The mural should be at least 400 sq. ft. in area (i.e. 20′ × 20′).
8. If the mural is a team adolescent mural, the youths are employed by the Department of Recreation and Parks at $2.47 per hour and the artist/director is responsible for their supervision (ask for additional information sheet for supervision).
9. Upon completion and approval of finished mural by members of the Mural Resource Center, the artist will receive $345.00 stipend. Signature of *all* participants should be placed on the wall.
10. With prior consent of the Mural Resource Center, a dedication ceremony can be held, honoring artist and participants, if you so desire.

DESIGN OF A TOMATO

The first chapter traced the origins of social design to the worldwide movement for human rights and environmental quality. Two specific intellectual currents, the civil rights movement and the environmental movement, were selected for expanded discussion. The consumer movement was a third force whose objectives and methods can be related to social design, but more for comparison than as a direct influence. A revival of the consumer movement occurred in the mid 1960s as a result of Ralph Nader's investigations into auto safety[1] and through the efforts of President John Kennedy to establish a consumer's bill of rights. This was the third resurgence of the consumer movement in the United States, the earlier two having occurred at 30-year intervals. In 1891 the Consumers League began in New York City, which affiliated in 1898 with the National Consumers League, the first national consumer organization in the United States. These organizations put strong pressure upon Congress, and with support from President Theodore Roosevelt, Congress passed the Pure Food Bill. A period of relative quiescence followed until 1927, when Stuart Chase and F. J. Schlink published *Your Money's Worth,*[2] which crystallized consumer discontent with shoddy products, false advertising, and high-pressure salesmanship. The book became an instant best seller and went through several editions. Responding to popular demands aroused by the book, Schlink established the first consumer testing agency to provide people with the technical information they needed to make their purchases.[3]

It is interesting to contrast social design with the revitalized consumer movement of the 1960s, with which it shared certain goals but used very different methods. The consumer movement focused its efforts on lobbying for protective legislation and on the complaint-handling process. It was a grassroots, action-oriented movement, different from an organization of professionals analyzing problems.[4] Its cardinal assumption was and is today that the consumers ultimately keep the marketplace honest. Self-regulation within the professions and government regulations are both necessary and desirable, but without a strong consumer presence, self-regulation and government will operate in the interests of industry. Special interest groups whose per capita benefits are sizeable will have more influence on regulatory bodies than the mass of consumers whose individual benefits are small. Regulatory agencies will therefore come under the control of the groups they are intended to regulate. Professional organizations can construct ethical codes in an attempt to keep practitioners responsible, but these organizations will tend to operate as guilds in furthering the interests of their membership. The consumer movement saw the solution as a combination of grassroots organization, lobbying, legislation, and product regulation.

Social design shared with the consumer movement a similar interest in product quality and industry accountability, but chose a very different strategy to achieve this. Whereas the consumer movement tried to intervene directly in the marketplace, social design was initiated and maintained at universities with the hope of influencing outside professional practice. Due to its roots in academe, social design remained apolitical. This avoidance of politics and direct consumer action can explain why social design faced little opposition while the consumer movement has faced considerable resistance throughout its existence. Consumer advocates were battling on the ramparts while social designers were giving lectures and doing research.

The consumer movement already shows signs of running out of steam as its intellectual capital is depleted. Arguments based on good intentions have an immediate short-run impact but little staying power. Social design attempted to generate concepts and methods, and rely on education and research as vehicles for change. This was not the grassroots education of the consumer movement, but the education of professionals in design and the behavioral sciences. The danger exists that social design will remain exclusively an academic enterprise whose influence is restricted to universities. Time will tell whether professional education and research without politics (social design) or politics and legislation without research (consumer movement) is the more successful strategy for improving product quality and increasing accountability within industry and the professions.

The present record of the social design movement can be judged in terms of impact upon awareness, methodology, and incentives. The first objective was raised awareness. Urban planners and architects had to be told of the implications of the separation between clients and users. Behavioral scientists needed to learn that the physical environment was an important determinant of behavior, that people did not float through life independent of their immediate surroundings. This goal was accomplished through articles, lectures, and personal encounters. As in the case of most programs aimed at increased awareness, the result was more successful on students and others whose careers were in flux than on established professionals. In terms of increased awareness, the social design movement is a success.

The second objective was to provide the concepts, tools, and techniques by which user participation and needs analysis could be accomplished. The result has been a rudimentary technology; many starts but little in the way of finished products. Techniques for statistical analysis are better developed than the instruments on which the measurements are based. There is room for considerable improvement in methods for assessing human response to the environment.

The third objective involved incentives for designers and clients to use available techniques for including user input. This raised the question of why an architect or building owner should hire a social scientist consultant or undergo the expense of evaluating completed projects. The answers thus far have been stated as moral imperatives, that is, it is good, desirable, professionally appropriate, and a necessary learning experience. In an era when design professionals are increasingly concerned about economic survival, such arguments may not be sufficient to change practice. As one cynic put it, truth and justice matter only if they benefit the client. A moral imperative functions only within the prevailing incentive system unless it can be institutionalized in rules, regulations, professional codes, and contractual obligations. Thus far the social design movement has not been very successful in developing incentives for practicing designers or their clients to include the new techniques in current projects.

NO NEW PROFESSION

Social design did not produce the new profession that many of its originators had visualized. The enduring theme of human culture is stability, not change. Nor did the pressures that were responsible for social design forge new professions among environmentalists and community organizers. Programs to train people for social change vocations faltered as outside funds dried up. The passion drained from community arts as federal grants were eliminated and programs cut. The strength and impact of all these movements is not seen in the emergence of independent professions but in the enlarged sense of responsibility for practitioners and in completed projects.

A few architects protested that young students were not

learning how to draw and that architecture with a capital *A* was being lost in the takeover of their field by other professions, but they had been saying this decades earlier.[5] Some behavioral scientists resented the intrusion of physical artifacts into abstract models and maintained that the discussion of situations diminished the generality of theories. Time has indicated that most of these fears were groundless. Architecture is back to form and the behavioral sciences are back to theory and research, but fortunately the fields are not where they were before. The change is in some measure due to the coming together of the two fields. The challenge today is to bring the new insights about people-place relationships into theories of human behavior and the processes by which neighborhoods and buildings are planned. Techniques such as user needs analysis and post-occupancy evaluation are steps in this direction, but the task of incorporating the results from their application into specific projects still remains.

It is still too early to rule out the possibility that a new profession will arise. Cornell University has developed a Facility Planning and Management Program, whose goal is to create a generalist whose education spans psychology, business, organizational behavior, and design. There are two new professional organizations (the National Association of Facility Planners and the Facility Planning and Management Association) and a new trade journal (*Facilities Design and Management*). The students entering this program are oriented not toward work with the practicing designer, but with corporate clients. Unlike previous waves of social scientists moving into the business community, these students will have a special concern with physical facility management and design.

Social design brought about changes in existing educational curricula and professional training. Most schools of planning and architecture have a social scientist to teach courses and advise students on research. This is a relatively new development. Twenty years ago I doubt if there was a single psychologist teaching full-time at a school of architecture. There are graduate programs within colleges of environmental design that emphasize human response to buildings. These programs are intended primarily for those who will teach and do research, but the existence of design faculty and students actively engaged in people-oriented research cannot help but penetrate the studios. In many cases the graduate students working for their advanced degrees in these programs will teach studio courses, and their enthusiasm for including occupant response will rub off on the undergraduate students.

The acceptance of a new outlook was not universal or total

in any of the professions, but there was an awareness that certain attitudes and approaches previously taken for granted were questionable if not indefensible (Table 5).

There is some truth in each of these statements, but it is an incomplete truth. While there might be some value in asking students to defend them as part of a mind-stretching exercise, these statements are not valid as the basis of professional practice.

The new approach within the social sciences introduced the physical environment into abstract theories of human activity. When I was in graduate school, there were frequent discussions

TABLE 5

Outmoded Attitudes

A. In Design

There is no way to gauge human response to buildings.

Architects should not care what the occupants think about a building. The views of clients, critics, and other architects are the only ones that matter.

There is nothing to be learned from the evaluation of completed projects.

The architect cannot be faulted if the occupants do not know how to use a building properly.

The designer is not responsible for the effects of a building on the surrounding neighborhood.

People don't know what they want in the way of architecture so there is no point in asking them.

The creation of beautiful form is the end product of all design.

B. In the Behavioral Sciences

People are not affected by their physical surroundings.

All the important things that happen in people's lives center on their relationships with other people.

Theories of human behavior can be stated in terms of personality and social systems irrespective of situations.

Human behavior can be properly studied only in the laboratory, where all relevant conditions can be controlled.

Neighborhood relationships can be understood and explained without considering the layout of interior and exterior spaces.

about the relative effects of heredity and environment, but environment meant family relationships and social roles. There was little attention to the physical artifacts of people's lives, except in anthropology, which tended to concern itself with primitive societies. Among the behavioral sciences, anthropology had the least difficulty in accommodating environmental concepts. On the debit side, anthropologists were not able to develop an applied technology to make their work immediately useful to designers. With the exception of salvage archaeology. anthropological field work in a setting remains a slow, laborious, and exhaustive process—the study of single places in fine detail—analogous to the archeologist's spending days digging out tiny pot shards from a square foot of earth.

The new approach meant bringing chairs and tables into the house of psychology. How demeaning it seemed for the developer of a grand theory of personality or social attraction to be asked to consider chairs and tables! Yet I defy anyone to explain interaction in a small group without knowing how the members are arranged spatially and whether they are seated or standing. As Roger Barker pointed out, the same person will behave very differently on a street corner and in a dentist's office.[6] Better predictions of people's behavior can be made from knowing the situations they are in than from data concerning their personality characteristics, occupation, or social class. Combined knowledge of situations and occupants and the connection between them is likely to yield the most accurate predictions of all.

As an academic specialty, social design is alive and healthy. Courses in Environmental Psychology or Sociology of the Environment are common in universities. More than 60 universities in the English-speaking world provide formal or informal graduate training in this specialty area. A dozen textbooks and six edited readers have been published on the topic.

There is half a division of the American Psychological Association devoted to environmental issues and an interest group of environmental sociologists, along with two professional organizations in the United States devoted to person-environment relationships—the Environmental Design Research Association (EDRA) and the Association for the Study of Man-Environment Relationships (ASMER). There are European counterparts to these associations and academic programs devoted to studying human response to the environment. There are also organized networks of researchers and practitioners concerned with specialized environmental issues. At least three periodicals are specifically dedicated to work in this field: *Environment and Behavior* in the United States, the *Journal of Environmental Psychology* in Great Britain, and *Architecture and Behavior* in Switzerland. The academic branch of the field is not without its problems, but they are similar to those encountered in any new field of study. The problems include a crisis of identity, resistance from entrenched disciplines who view any new program as a drain upon available resources, doubts among funding agencies about whether this is a legitimate and fruitful area of study, uncertainty among publishers regarding potential markets, and a gulf between theory and practice.

The epistemological base of the field is securely grounded. A research tradition is gradually being accepted which will enrich existing programs. The title "research architect" or "design researcher" still does not evoke an image. This will change as research becomes a legitimate and even a required part of the duties of architecture and planning faculty. Not all designers will choose to work on behavioral issues, of course, but some will. Behavioral research is but one among several valid research options in design. Other approaches are even more appropriate to some issues, including historical research, which is required in neighborhood preservation, the taxonomy of forms, styles and periods, documentation through photography and other media, and materials research, where design intersects with engineering. At some point all of these topics have behavioral implications, but specific portions of the research, such as the analysis of materials' strength or flammability, is not behavioral. However, once designers become involved in any type of research, the search for new knowledge becomes contagious and creates a "questioning community" in which the behavioral implications must be considered.

An urgent need in the spread of building evaluation and needs analysis is for standardized instruments that can be used in a variety of settings. Presently each person who evaluates a building tends to invent questions and develop homemade questionnaires. Not only is this wasted effort, since others have probably developed similar methods, but it rules out the possibility of comparing the results across different settings. Instruments can be developed from existing theories of people-place relationships and eventually will enrich those theories and develop new theories. Standardized instruments will also add to the generality of findings across geographic areas. Presently there is little collaboration among researchers in different regions. It would be useful to compare the evaluation of high-rise apartment buildings in cities as different as Boston, Milan, and Leningrad. Cooperation among researchers in different regions can enrich the data base out of which theories of people-place relationships are developed.

As a college instructor, I had a personal interest in career opportunities that might emerge from the linkage between behavioral sciences and design. Students were writing to me from afar to ask about possible jobs in this new specialty. The early hope that a new profession would be created midway between architecture and the behavioral sciences went unrealized. There was not a sufficient economic base for a new vocation. It had been naively assumed that if the need for services were clearly described, someone would come up with the money. Clients of multi-million dollar projects were expected to recognize the value of spending a small amount of money to bring in a social scientist to conduct a user needs analysis. The logic of this argument proved more compelling to academics than to those familiar with the economics of the construction industry. A multi-million dollar budget for a new building seems large in relation to a thousand dollar consultant fee until it is broken down into its various components. If the consultant's fee were to come out of the architect's 5 percent of the budget, it was no longer play money, but actual dollars of significant magnitude.

It was hoped that designers would be able to sell clients on the need for behavioral consultation once they themselves were convinced of its worth. This was the assumption of those of us who attempted to reach urban planners and architects through talks at professional meetings, journal articles, and visiting lectures. Had the building boom continued, this indirect approach might have had a better chance of success. As competition for contracts increased and new demands were placed on practitioners by federal, state, and local regulations, there was little inclination to sell clients on the value of a new service. Some offices, such as Gerald Davis in Vancouver and Kaplan and McLaughlin in San Francisco, found that needs analysis and post-occupancy evaluation are important activities that can be sold to some clients some of the time, but not on a regular basis that could justify career-track employees.

Proponents of the original dream could maintain that the time was not right for a new profession. Social design came into its own when the construction boom was ending, when money began to dry up, and new regulations increased the complexity of the planning process. The day was hardly auspicious for a new consultant who would add to the budget and raise issues that were not being considered by the client or required by government regulations. The timing was not good, to be sure, but I suspect that the timing is always less than ideal. As a character in Sartre's *No Exit* declared, "One always dies too soon or too late."

In answering queries from students or practitioners regarding jobs in this field, I give different answers to those from the behavioral sciences and those from the design fields. For those in architecture, I agree with Neal Deasy, one of the first practicing architects to apply a social design approach, that the student should become competent in practical design, obtain employment doing design work, and then seek contact with a nearby social scientist. A course in the sociology of the environment or environmental psychology at a college is a good indication of the presence of an interested faculty member. If there is a school of architecture or planning, the existence of an interested social scientist is almost a certainty. Full-fledged collaboration must await the right sort of project. It probably will not be an ideal project with ample time and resources for collaboration, but one with a client open to behavioral issues and willing to invest a small amount of time, money, and effort in examining occupant responses.

The future seems a little brighter than the present in this regard, as those professionals trained in a social design approach become principals in their own firms and can hire social scientists, recruit clients willing to include a social scientist on projects, and squeeze out time and resources from the firm to investigate the behavioral aspects of current projects. An alternative that I do *not* recommend is for design students to bypass traditional practice and begin work for a university or nonprofit agency engaged in research or consultation. I am skeptical about the value of what the Chinese describe as the three-door approach, a young person's leaving the door of the home to enter the door of the school and eventually entering the door of a government office without being exposed to the outside world. Some acquaintance with actual practice will be invaluable even for those whose primary interests are in teaching and research.

For students from the behavioral sciences, I recommend one of the new specialty programs in this area.[7] For employability, specialization by topical area is a requirement. This is difficult for me to say with conviction because I am a generalist at heart. The sociologist who becomes knowledgeable in recreation or wilderness experience can find opportunities in park planning at the local, state, or federal level. One of my former students teaches in a natural resources program. The psychologist willing to learn about the environmental needs of the handicapped may be able to find a position with an agency or organization concerned with physical disability. If demographics is any guide, the environmental needs of the elderly is a growth area. Sadly, there is a current boom in correctional architecture. I do not view specialization as a straitjacket that can never be removed. Topical areas overlap and there are natural connections. The design of a proper chair eventually connects to desks, tables, and offices. There is an easy transition from the study of parks and plazas to city streets. Learning about one issue will be helpful in dealing with another, although the differences must also be recognized. There are some academic programs that deal with general categories of buildings, such as the Cornell Program in Facility Management and Planning, that may provide entry to a range of positions within the business community.

Graduates of these programs have been getting good jobs, many of which are not in academe. Few graduates of the CUNY Environmental Psychology Program have taken academic positions. Some have obtained influential positions with private developers and government agencies, often finding themselves clients for architects and designers. Examples include Marilyn Rothenberg, who is a high-level administrator for the Children's Television Workshop, for whom she directs their "Sesame Place Theme Park," including projects involving millions of dollars in construction budgets and architect's fees; Rich Olsen, who is Director of Research and in charge of a major renovation effort for Bellevue Hospital in New York City, and Lisa Cashden, who directs the New York City Land Program for the Trust for Public Land.

Not all of these positions are involved with new construction. Management and renovation require different sorts of expertise. For many clients, renovation is a more feasible option than new construction. The high cost of land, materials, labor, energy, and borrowed money make it more economical to rehabilitate than to build and move. Most work in park planning involves ways to make existing parks more habitable and appropriate to leisure activities. Home owners are not buying and selling houses as often as they did in the past decades. Eventually the United States will become more like Europe, where successive generations occupy the same residence and work in the same commercial establishments. Renovation has the ecological advantage of reusing existing materials and structures. An architect can earn a good fee by advising occupants how to get the most out of their present buildings, to improve the quality of space, and reduce expenditures for energy.

DESIGN OF A TOMATO

There is always room in a book about design for a good tomato story. In 1969 I ended *Personal Space*[8] with an account of the tough, tasteless, square tomato that growers had developed to withstand machine handling, to stack easily, and still retain good appearance and long shelf life. This was only one of many examples of the quest to rebuild organisms to fit technology. Plant geneticists worked for years to create special blunt-ended carrots that would not perforate polyethylene bags. In the end, the geneticists' labors proved unnecessary; the makers of polyethylene bags came up with a tougher plastic.[9] Square apple trees are being developed to match machines that can prune them and pluck their fruit. Agricultural engineer Bernard Tennes proudly declared, "The day of the square apple tree is coming. Instead of designing equipment to suit the shape of fruit trees, we should shape the trees to suit new, more efficient machines."[10] Turkeys are being bred to fit refrigerators, corn to match harvesting machines, and mini-poodles for mini-apartments. At one point, officials of the Chicago and Southern Airlines broadcast a call for stewardesses no taller than four feet ten inches. The reason was that cabin ceilings in their commuter aircraft were only five feet high.[11]

The thrust of such policies is that technology comes before people. The freight train moves speedily through the intersection while the passenger train waits on the siding. The architectural analogy is that people should adapt to their buildings. There is no doubt that *homo sapiens* is an extremely flexible species. If people

FIGURES 23, 24, 25 The frontier of social design lies more in renovation than in new construction. Here is a bar converted into an attractive and popular senior center (Figure 23), an A&W root beer stand recycled into a distinctive seafood restaurant (Figure 24), and a 7–11 store transformed into a children's dental clinic (Figure 25).

23

24

25

FIGURE 26 Jersey tomato T-shirt. Relic of an era when the New Jersey tomato was the standard of quality in the industry.

FIGURE 27 Roadside stands kept alive customers' memories of flavorful tomatoes.

FIGURE 28 Buyer resistance induced researchers to use consumer panels to improve fresh tomato flavor.

can live in the arid Sahara and among Arctic snows, surely they can learn to bend over when they enter small aircraft, carry cushions to their offices if the chairs are uncomfortable, shut out urban noise, and ignore ugly buildings. Certainly most people *can* adapt themselves to all these conditions and worse. The question is whether they should. There will always be compromises between economics, technology, and human needs, but the system of priorities has to be set straight.

My account of the tough, tasteless, square tomato proved prescient. Within a few years, there was a great public outcry about tomatoes.[12] The tomato industry had moved west to California and somewhere along the interstate, flavor was lost. Maybe it dropped off in Michigan or Wisconsin. When tomatoes in my part of California fall from a truck, they bounce. Growers claim this is only true of canning tomatoes, yet consumer response to supermarket tomatoes says otherwise. Among Florida tomatoes, the pride of the agricultural laboratories was MH-1, legendary in farm circles because it could be dropped ripe from a height of six feet without breaking.[13] A tomato receiver who was interviewed by a reporter for a trade journal and who asked not to be identified, declared, "Everybody knows Florida tomatoes are good, and they never get soft."[14]

According to surveys made by the U.S. Department of Agriculture, there is more consumer dissatisfaction over fresh tomato flavor than with any other fresh fruit or vegetable.[15] Food critics have made similar complaints. Craig Claiborne, food editor for the

New York Times, calls store tomatoes "tasteless, hideous, and repulsive." "Inedible," says author Edward Giobbi. "They are like eating a blotter,"[16] Thomas Whiteside finds that, "Instead of the simple, fragrant, tender, juicy, and glorious tasting fruit we once knew, we see (in the supermarket) stacks of boxes containing sets of three or four pinkish globes, still pallid after their stay in the (ethylene) gas chamber, resting peacefully in their plastic tubes, each of them embalmed in a thin coat of wax for cosmetic effect, and all uniformly dry, mealy, insipid."[17]

The new strawberry also has its critics. People complain that today's berries taste like potatoes and bounce like rubber balls. The strawberry of the future is expected to be even sturdier. According to Herb Baum, the chief operating officer of the Natureripe Berry Growers Cooperative, a shipper must assume that the worst will happen and that the crates will be handled roughly and be improperly refrigerated. "You have to come up with something that is a hardware item," Baum declared, "otherwise the shrinkage is so great that the chain stores won't want to handle the berries." One of the new varieties being prepared for market is described by another major strawberry grower as "sour, pithy, and hollow. It's a tough mother, but these shippers love it. It's the worst-tasting and the fastest-growing in popularity among growers. You ship this to New York City and you know it's going to get there, and that's money in the grower's pocket."[18]

These situations resulted from the neglect of consumer opinion by growers, processors, and the agricultural scientists who developed the new varieties to emphasize toughness, long shelf life, and good appearance at the expense of tenderness, freshness, and taste. Jerry Brownstein, executive vice president of Embassy Produce, the biggest distributor of fresh market tomatoes in the New York area stated, "The important thing for us in a tomato is to get it to the consumer looking good. No blemishes, no black spots, no softness."[19] Among the variety of store (*not* cannery) fruit being prepared for machine harvesting are "jointless tomatoes." Without joints on the stems, the fruit can be plucked right off the plant and lifted onto the machine. After the tomatoes are swept into the harvester, a knife cuts off the plant, and the tomatoes are delivered on top of iron "shakers" that shake the dirt and the vines off the tomatoes. After the tomatoes are sorted and washed, they are swept up on another elevator and dumped into a bin or trailer. Then they are stored in a packing house for a week or two until they are shipped out.[20]

In the face of mounting public criticism, each group vehemently denied responsibility for the situation. Growers protested that they were only delivering what the retailer wanted—an attractive product with long shelf life—and retailers said that the present system gave the customer year-round availability of fresh produce, while the agricultural scientists maintained that they were only responding to industry demands. Eventually growers, wholesalers, shippers, and retailers joined in the familiar refrain of blaming the victim. It was all the consumer's fault for wanting year-round availability of unblemished fresh market tomatoes. The fact that consumers were voting with their pocketbooks to boycott the tasteless leather-jacketed products of the new agriculture and took to gardening and buying from small farmers raised important questions about the accuracy of the industry view.

Fortunately our story does not end at this point. Buyer resistance inspired the tomato industry to seek new varieties with good flavor as well as good appearance and long shelf life. The resistance would not have materialized if the public had not retained some contact with good-tasting tomatoes, due in large measure to the efforts of small farmers and home gardeners. As long as a person could recall eating a fresh juicy, tender tomato, the fluorescent variety of the supermarket seemed more suited for the playing field than the dinner table.

Tasteless fruit helped to boost home gardening and farmers' markets. All across the United States, farmers' markets are springing up in which small growers sell fresh local produce directly to consumers. The chief motivation on the part of the consumer, as revealed in more than a half-dozen surveys in as many different states of the union, is not lower prices but improved food quality, as indicated by better freshness and flavor.[21] Customers are willing to engage in slightly less convenient shopping to obtain good tasting corn, bell peppers, and tomatoes. Their behavior contradicts the widely held assumption in the restaurant industry that most Americans do not care about their vegetables. The understandable explanation is that people, unless they are starving, will not value tasteless, overcooked and insipid food.

Buyer resistance made the industry aware of the problems with the tough, tasteless, square tomato. Consumer tests were conducted on new varieties to improve flavor, texture, and overall palatability. Applying this model to the building industry poses certain problems. In an ideal world, there would be consumer tests of new architectural prototypes. Designs would be tried out and evaluated before they were used on the public. Unfortunately, the decentralized nature of design practice and the expense of test buildings precludes the use of full-scale prototypes in most situations. Techniques such as simulation, needs analysis, POE, and direct involvement of users in the design process must substitute for full-scale test buildings.

For millions of occupants of uncomfortable and nonfunctional buildings, the prospect of a more rational design process in the future offers little immediate relief. Most people cannot boycott spaces that they do not like. If the building in which they live or work is tough, tasteless, and square, they are unable to avoid it. The solution in such cases is to brighten and humanize the interiors and prevent more construction of this type through raised awareness among owners, designers, and occupants.

NOTES

CHAPTER 1

1. Wolf Von Eckhardt, "The Age of Anti-architecture," *Saturday Review,* January 23, 1965, p. 19.
2. Henry Dreyfuss, "Industrial Design," *Encyclopedia Yearbook,* (1964), 158–259.
3. Rudolf Arnheim, *The Dynamics of Architectural Form* (Berkeley: CA: University of California Press, 1977), p. 3.
4. Philip Thiel, "Architects, Clients, Purposes and Power" (unpublished paper, April 1977), p. 4.
5. Douglas Davis, "New Architecture," *Newsweek,* April 19, 1971, p. 78.
6. Arnheim, *Dynamics of Architectural Form.*
7. The opposite approach characterizes advertising, where it is extremely rare to find a scene without people. Even a landscape or nature view will have some person or person-surrogate to catch the viewer's eye. Advertising copywriters are aware that pictures of other people are more interesting to readers than anything else. This could justify the practice of excluding people from architectural photographs on the grounds that people would distract attention from the building. The weakness of this argument, as Arnheim indicates, is that except for certain monuments, the presence of people is an inextricable part of our experience of buildings. In addition, the practice of excluding people increases the risks that the building will ignore human scale and those amenities that occupants appreciate.
8. Simon Nicholson and Barbara K. Schreiner, *Community Participation in City Decision Making,* (Milton Keynes, UK: Open University Press, 1973), p. 8.
9. Michel Seuphor, *Piet Mondrian,* (New York: Abrams, n.d.).
10. Richard Neutra, *Survival Through Design,* (New York: Oxford University Press, 1954), p. vii.
11. Amos Rapoport, "An Interview on Vernacular Architecture," *Jour. of the Faculty of Architecture, 5,* Middle East Technical University (1979), p. 116.
12. Mark Francis, "Reflections On Community Design," paper presented at National Conference on Participatory Design in Low Income Communities, American Institute of Architects, Washington, D.C., October 26–27, 1982.
13. Rachel Carson, *Silent Spring,* (Boston: Houghton Mifflin, 1962).
14. Michael McCloskey, "Editorial," *Sierra Club Bulletin,* (June 1970), p. 2.

15. David A. Aaker and George S. Day, *Consumerism: Search for the Consumer Interest,* 2nd ed., (New York: Free Press, 1974), p. xx.
16. Danielle Starkey, "Author Addresses Hunger Problem," *The California Aggie,* (Davis, CA, June 7, 1982), p. 1.
17. Quoted in François Choay, *Le Corbusier* (New York: George Braziller, 1960), p. 18.
18. F. J. Langdon, "The Social and Physical Environment: A Social Scientist's View," *R.I.B.A. Jour. 73* (October 1966), p. 462.
19. Douglas Davis, "New Architecture," *Newsweek,* April 19, 1971, p. 78.
20. Neutra, *Survival Through Design.*

CHAPTER 2

1. Amos Rapoport, *House Form and Culture* (Englewood Cliffs: Prentice-Hall, 1969).
2. David Stea, "The Three-P's of Environmental Cognition: Perception, Positivism, and Participation," *Jour. of the Faculty of Architecture, 6,* Middle East Technical University (1980), 101–128.
3. N. Tinbergen, *Social Behavior in Animals* (London: Methuen, 1953); H. Hediger, *Studies of the Psychology and Behavior of Captive Animals in Zoos and Circuses* (London: Butterworths, 1955).
4. Humphry Osmond, "Function as the Basis of Psychiatric Ward Design," *Mental Hospitals* (April 1957), pp. 23–29.
5. E. T. Hall, *The Silent Language* (Garden City, NY: Doubleday, 1959).
6. E. Goffman, *Behavior in Public Places* (Glencoe: Free Press, 1963).
7. R. G. Barker, "Explorations in Ecological Psychology," *American Psychologist,* 20 (1965), pp. 1–14.
8. K. Lynch, *The Image of the City* (Cambridge: The Technology Press, 1960).
9. Philip Thiel, "Notes on the Description, Scaling, Notation, and Scoring of Some Perceptual and Cognitive Attributes of the Physical Environment," in *Environmental Psychology,* ed. H. H. Proshansky, et al., (New York: Holt, Rinehart, and Winston, 1970), pp. 593–619.
10. Christopher Alexander, et al., *A Pattern Language* (New York: Oxford University Press, 1977).
11. Donald Appleyard and Kenneth Craik, "The Berkeley Environmental Simulation Project," in *Environmental Impact Assessment,* eds. T. G. Dickert and K. R. Domeny (Berkeley: University of California Extension, 1974), pp. 121–126. Also Alton DeLong, "The Use of Scale Models in Spatial Behavioral Research," *Man-Environment Systems, 6* (1976), pp. 179–182.
12. D. E. Berlyne, ed., *Studies in the New Experimental Aesthetics* (New York: Halsted, 1974).
13. R. Kaplan, "Some Methods and Strategies in the Prediction of Preference," in *Landscape Assessment,* E. H. Zube, J. G. Fabos, and R. O. Brush, eds. (Stroudsburg, PA: Dowden, Hutchinson, and Ross, 1974).

14. T. C. Daniel and R. S. Boster, "Measuring Landscape Aesthetics," *U.S.D.A. Forest Service,* paper RM-167 (1976).

15. M. P. Lawton, "Therapeutic Environments for the Aged," in *Designing for Therapeutic Environments,* D. Canter and S. Canter, eds. (Chichester, England: Wiley, 1979).

16. Franklin D. Becker, *Housing Messages* (Stroudsburg, PA: Dowden, Hutchinson, and Ross, 1977).

17. J. Farbstein, "A Juvenile Services Center Program," in *Facility Programming,* Wolfgang Preiser, ed. (Stroudsburg, Pa.: Dowden, Hutchinson, and Ross, 1978).

18. Robert Sommer and Bonnie Kroll, "Mental Patients and Nurses Rate Habitability," in *Designing for Therapeutic Environments,* D. Canter and S. Canter, eds. (Sussex, UK: Wiley, 1979), pp. 199–212.

19. I. L. McHarg, *Design with Nature* (Garden City, NY: Natural History Press, 1969).

20. Emile Durkheim, *Suicide* (Glencoe, IL: Free Press, 1951).

21. Oscar Newman, *Defensible Space* (New York: The MacMillan Company, 1972).

22. Barker, *Ecological Psychology.*

23. ERDF, "Arrowhead: Final Recommendations" (Kansas City: Environmental Research and Development Foundation, 1971).

24. Paul Goodman, "Conversations," *Psychology Today* (November 1971), p. 96.

25. Mark Francis, Lisa Cashdan, and Lynn Paxson, *The Making of Neighborhood Open Spaces* (New York: Center for Human Environments, City University of New York, April 1981).

26. K. Lewin, *Resolving Social Conflicts* (New York: Harper & Bros., 1948).

27. John Zeisel, *Inquiry by Design* (Monterey, CA: Brooks/Cole, 1981); R. Sommer and Barbara B. Sommer, *A Practical Guide to Behavioral Research* (New York: Oxford University Press, 1980).

CHAPTER 3

1. Daniel Stokols, "Environmental Psychology," *Annual Review of Psychology, 29* (1978), pp. 253–295.

2. David Canter, *The Psychology of Place* (London: Architectural Press, 1977), p. ix.

3. K. Lewin, *A Dynamic Theory of Personality* (New York: McGraw-Hill, 1935).

4. K. Helphand, "Environmental Autobiography," Paper presented at the International Conference on Environmental Psychology at the University of Surrey (July 1979).

5. Leonard Krasner, ed. *Environmental Design and Human Behavior* (New York: Pergamon, 1980).

6. John D. Cone and Steven C. Hayes, *Environmental Problems/Behavioral Solutions* (Monterey, CA: Brooks/Cole, 1980).

7. Ibid.
8. Philip M. Boffey, "A Scientist Looks Within to See the Effects of Aging," *Sacramento Bee,* August 31, 1982, p. B4.
9. Berlyne, *Experimental Aesthetics.*
10. J. J. Gibson, *The Senses Considered as Perceptual Systems* (Boston: Houghton Mifflin, 1966).
11. Osmond, Ward Design.
12. Newman, *Defensible Space.*
13. Lynch, *Image of the City.*
14. M. L. J. Abercrombie, "Psychology and the Architectural Student," Talk given at the Conference on Architectural Psychology, Park City, UT (May 28, 1966).
15. Seymour M. Gold, "Nonuse of Neighborhood Parks," *Jour. of the American Institute of Planners, 38* (1972), pp. 369–378.
16. G. O. Handegord and N. B. Hutcheon, "The Use of Test Buildings in Building Research," Technical paper Number 104, Division of Building Research (Ottawa, Canada, 1960).
17. Osmond, Ward Design.
18. "Food Retailing—A Restless, Ever-Changing Business," *Progressive Grocer* (October 1952), p. 64.
19. Hiroshi Isogai and Shunjiro Matsushima, *Market Places of the World* (Palo Alto, CA: Kodansha International Limited, 1972).
20. Joe Carcione and Bob Lucas, *The Greengrocer* (San Francisco, CA: Chronicle Books, 1972).
21. Paul N. Bloom and Steven A. Greyser, "Exploring the Future of Consumerism," *Marketing Science Institute,* Report No. 81–102 (July 1981).
22. Rom J. Markin, *The Supermarket: An Analysis of Growth, Development, and Change,* Rev. ed. (Pullman, WA: Washington State University Press, 1968).
23. Robert Sommer, John Herrick, and Ted R. Sommer, "The Behavioral Ecology of Supermarkets and Farmers' Markets," *Jour. of Environmental Psychology, 1,* (1981), pp. 13–19.
24. Elizabeth A. Schiferl and Robert D. Boynton, "A Comparative Performance Analysis of New Wave Retail Food Cooperatives and Private Food Stores," Agricultural Experiment Station Bulletin No. 380 (Dept. of Agricultural Economics, Purdue University, West Lafayette, IN, June 1982).
25. Robert Sommer and Marcia Horner, "Social Interaction in Co-ops and Supermarkets," *Communities, 49* (1981), pp. 15–18.
26. Sommer, Herrick, and Sommer. "Behavioral Ecology."
27. Le Corbusier, *The Radiant City* (London: Faber, 1967).
28. Newman, *Defensible Space.*
29. Ibid.
30. C. Ray Jeffery, *Crime Prevention Through Environmental Design,* 2nd ed., (Beverly Hills, CA: Sage, 1977).

31. Timothy D. Crowe, et al., *Crime Prevention Through Environmental Design: School Demonstration Plan Broward County, Florida* (Arlington, VA: Westinghouse Electric Corporation, March 1976), p. xxi.

CHAPTER 4

1. N. Sanford, "Whatever Happened to Action Research?" *Jour. of Social Issues, 26* (1970), p. 10.
2. R. G. Barker, *Psychological Ecology* (Stanford, CA: Stanford University Press, 1968).
3. Rudolf Moos, *Evaluating Treatment Environments* (New York: Wiley, 1974), p. 2.
4. Harold M. Proshansky, "Methodology in Environmental Psychology: Problems and Issues," *Human Factors, 14*(5) (1972), p. 459.
5. R. Hogan, "Interview," *APA Monitor* (April 1979), p. 4.
6. R. Widgery and C. Stackpole, "Desk Position, Interviewee Anxiety, and Interviewer Credibility," *Jour. of Counselling Psychology, 19,* 1972), pp. 173–177; William P. Ryan, "Therapist's Office as a Treatment Variable," *Psychological Reports, 45* (1979), pp. 671–675.
7. Any discussion of the motives that bring people into a field necessarily oversimplifies a complex situation. There were some social scientists who became interested in environmental issues to enrich existing theories, and there were some architects and landscape designers whose interest in person-environment transactions was to provide a new service that might attract new clients and new commissions.
8. Roger Bailey, Personal Communication (1980).
9. David Canter, "Empirical Research in Environmental Psychology," *Bulletin of the British Psychological Society, 27* (1974), p. 35.

CHAPTER 5

1. Ada Louise Huxtable, "The Art We Cannot Afford to Ignore (But Do)," *New York Times Magazine* (May 4, 1958), pp. 14–15.
2. Numerous alternatives to laboratory experimentation have been proposed within the social sciences that do not require full control over all variables and the random assignment of people to treatment conditions. These quasi-experiments, natural experiments, or ex post facto experiments as they are often called, allow researchers to investigate problems that cannot be brought into the laboratory. Even here, the size and expense of physical systems and time pressures do not allow the continuous variation and the replication required by the laboratory standard of scientific proof. This does not rule out the possibility of experimentation in design. The point is that such experimentation will rarely reach laboratory standards of proof.

3. Carol Weinstein, "Modifying Student Behavior in an Open Classroom Through Changes in Physical Design," *American Educational Research Jour., 14* (1977), pp. 249–262.
4. M. Kay Harris and Dudley P. Spiller, Jr., *After Decision: Implementation of Judicial Decrees in Correctional Settings* (Washington, D.C., LEAA, U.S. Dept. of Justice, October 1977).
5. Charles J. Holahan and Susan Saegert, "Behavioral and Attitudinal Effects of Large-Scale Variation on the Physical Environment of Psychiatric Wards," *Jour. of Abnormal Psychology, 82*(3) (1973), pp. 454–462. Toni Farrenkopf, "Man-Environment Interaction: An Academic Department Moves Into a New Building," (Ph.D. dissertation, University of Mass., 1974).
6. Kathryn H. Anthony, "Form Follows Needs: Non-Traditional Design at Patrick Sullivan Associates," (Unpublished Report, 1982).
7. John Ruskin, *The Two Paths* (New York: John Wiley, 1859), p. 124.
8. Frank Becker, Personal Communication. Additional information about the effects of office environment on morale are contained in Professor Becker's book, *Workspace* (New York: Praeger, 1981).
9. Joan Solomon, "So Human a Science," *The Sciences, 10*(11) (November 1970), pp. 28–30.
10. Carter Wiseman, "Architecture's Master of the Middle Way," *Saturday Review,* November 1981, p. 24.
11. Arnheim, *Dynamics of Architectural Form,* p. 7.

CHAPTER 6

1. Arnheim, *Dynamics of Architectural Form,* p. 7.
2. T. Scitovsky, *The Joyless Economy* (New York: Oxford University Press), 1976.
3. Franklin D. Becker, *User Participation, Personalization and Environmental Meaning* (Ithaca, New York: Cornell University Program in Urban and Regional Studies, 1977).
4. L. Halprin, *Cities* (Cambridge, MA: MIT Press, 1972).
5. C. M. Deasy, *Design for Human Affairs* (New York: John Wiley, 1974), p. 77.
6. Kathryn Anthony, "Form Follows Needs."
7. Gerald Davis "What Is New About Building Programming?" Address given to the Building Research Institute (Anaheim, CA, September 18–19, 1968).
8. F. J. Roethlisberger and W. J. Dickson, *Management and the Worker* (Cambridge, Mass.: Harvard University Press, 1939).
9. Rachel Kaplan, "Citizen Participation in the Design and Evaluation of a Park," *Environment and Behavior, 12* (1980), pp. 494–507.
10. Robert Sommer, "Floor Designs Can Be Therapeutic," *Hospitals, 34* (December 16, 1960), pp. 54–56.

11. Robert Sommer and Helge Olsen, "The Soft Classroom," *Environment and Behavior, 12* (1980), pp. 3–16.
12. Walter Kleeman, "The Quiet Battle," *Furniture Manufacturing Management* (September 1980), pp. 13–14.
13. Needs analysis can also be done as a class project. When this occurs, it is important to explain to occupants that the survey may not change their situation. This admission may diminish participation, but it is required by research ethics. Training is a valid activity and building occupants are likely to answer questions on this basis alone. My own students have been able to obtain good cooperation when they interviewed people in many different types of buildings, even though the interview was described as a class exercise.
14. W. Gibbs and R. W. Cramer, "Dining Facility User-Attitudes and Environmental Design Research at Travis Air Force Base, California," *Preliminary Report D-5* (Construction Engineering Research Laboratory, Champaign, IL, 1973); W. Gibbs, "Comparative Study of Consumer Attitudes at Three Air Force Dining Facilities," *Interim Report D-40* (Construction Engineering Research Laboratory, Champaign, IL, 1974).
15. D. L. Dressel, et al., "Army Family Housing: Preferences and Attitudes About Housing Interiors, Vol. 1," *Technical Report D-48* (Construction Engineering Research Laboratory, February 1975).

CHAPTER 7

1. Rapoport, Interview.
2. William H. Whyte, *The Social Life of Small Urban Spaces* (New York: The Conservation Foundation, 1980).
3. Environmental Design Research Association, Inc., L'Enfant Plaza Station, P.O. Box 23129, Washington, D.C., 20024.
4. John Howard, *The State of the Prisons in England and Wales, Etc.* (London: Warrington, 1777).
5. Thomas Kirkbride, *On the Construction, Organization, and General Arrangement of Hospitals for the Insane* (Philadelphia: Lindsay and Blakiston, 1854).
6. Aaron Cohen and Elaine Cohen, *Designing and Space Planning for Libraries* (New York: R. R. Bowker, 1979).
7. These three accounts were written expressly for this volume.

CHAPTER 8

1. Simon Nicholson and Barbara K. Schreiner, *Community Participation in City Decision Making* (Milton Keynes, UK: Open University Press, 1976).
2. Amos Rapoport, *House Form and Culture* (Englewood Cliffs, NJ: Prentice-Hall, 1969).

3. Rapoport, Interview, p. 122.
4. Rapoport, *House Form and Culture,* p. 5.
5. Ibid, p. 6.
6. Nicholson and Schreiner, *Community Participation.*
7. Simon Nicholson, "The Theory of Loose Parts," *Landscape Architecture Quarterly, 62* (1971), pp. 30–34.
8. Rapoport, Interview, p. 123.
9. J. Turner, *Housing by People* (New York: Pantheon, 1976).
10. F. D. Becker, *Housing Messages* (Stroudsburg, PA: Dowden, Hutchinson, and Ross, 1977).
11. Kaplan, Participation in Environmental Design.
12. Becker, *Housing Messages.*
13. C. Alexander, M. Silverstein, S. Angel, S. Ishikawa, and D. Abrams, *The Oregon Experiment* (New York: Oxford, 1975).
14. Bernard Rudofsky, *Architecture Without Architects* (Garden City, New York: Doubleday, 1964).
15. Mark Francis, "Designing Landscapes with Community Participation and Behavioral Research," *Landscape Architectural Forum* (Spring 1982), pp. 15–39.
16. Nicholson and Schreiner, *Community Participation.*
17. Henry Sanoff, "Games for User Participation, in *Designing the Method,* D. K. Tester, ed. (Raleigh, N.C.: Student Publication of the School of Design, North Carolina State University, 1974).
18. L. Halprin, *The RSVP Cycles* (New York: Braziller, 1969).
19. Robert Sommer, *Design Awareness* (San Francisco: Rinehart, 1972), p. 44.
20. Alexander, et al., *The Oregon Experiment.*
21. Marjie Lambert, "Placerville Nurses Helped Design New Hospital Wing," *Sacramento Bee,* August 29, 1982, p. B4.
22. David Bainbridge, Judy Corbett, and John Hofacre, *Village Homes' Solar House Design* (Emmaus, PA: Rodale Press, 1979). See also Michael Corbett, *A Better Place to Live* (Emmaus, PA: Rodale Press, 1981).
23. William Michelson, "Most People Don't Want What Architects Want," *Trans-Action* (July/August, 1968), pp. 37–43.
24. Robert Sommer, "Participatory Design," *Ideas* (August 1979), pp. 4–5.

CHAPTER 9

1. Walter Kleeman, "Some Notes on the Future of Chairs," *Furniture Manufacturing Management* (February 1979), pp. 26–27.
2. Min Kantrowitz and Richard Nordhaus, "The Impact of Post-Occupancy Evaluation Research," *Environment and Behavior, 12* (1980), pp. 508–519.

3. Farrenkopf, Dissertation.

4. Yvonne A. W. Clearwater, "Social-Environmental Relationships in Open and Closed Offices (Unpublished Ph.D. Thesis, University of California, Davis, 1979).

5. Schuyler Ingle, "Secrets of the Earth," *New West* (July 1981), p. 128.

6. Martha M. Hamilton, "Facing the Green Glow in the Office," *Sacramento Bee* (September 6, 1981), p. AA 1.

7. Scott Fitzgerald, "The Crackup," *Esquire* (February 1982), p. 74 (orig. pub. 1936).

8. Kaplan, "Citizen Participation."

9. Walter B. Kleeman, Jr., *The Challenge of Interior Design* (Boston: CBI Publishing, 1981).

10. C. M. Zimring and J. E. Reizenstein, "Post-Occupancy Evaluation: An Overview," *Environment and Behavior, 12* (1980), pp. 429–450.

11. Carter Wiseman, "Why Is Everyone Talking About Michael Graves?" *Saturday Review* (March 1982), p. 41.

12. Ingle, Secrets of the Earth, p. 128.

13. John Goodman and Marc Grainer, *Consumer Complaint Handling in America: Final Report,* Prepared for U.S. Office of Consumer Affairs (September 1979).

14. "Putting Excellence into Management," *Business Week* (July 21, 1980), pp. 196–197.

15. John A. Goodman and Larry M. Robinson, "Strategies for Improving the Satisfaction of Business Customers," *Business, 32* (1982), pp. 40–44.

16. Measuring the Grapevine—Consumer Response and Word-of-Mouth," Consumer Information Center (The Coca-Cola Company, Atlanta, Georgia, 1981).

17. R. B. Bechtel, and R. K. Srivastava "Post-Occupancy Evaluation of Housing," (Unpublished Report, 1978).

18. L. Wheeler, *Behavioral Research for Architectural Planning and Design* (Terre Haute, IN: Ewing Miller Associates, 1967).

19. Gordon Allport, *Pattern and Growth in Personality* (New York: Holt, Rinehart, and Winston, 1961).

20. Becker, *Housing Messages.*

21. Sommer, *Design Awareness.*

22. Michael Durkin and Robert Sommer, "User Evaluation of Three Branch Libraries," *California Librarian* (April 1972), pp. 114–123.

23. Deasy, Bolling, and Gill, Architects, "A Study of Community Attitudes for the Los Angeles Library System," (Unpublished Report, 1974).

24. David Canter, et al., *Prison Design and Use Study: Final Report* (Psychology Department, University of Surrey, September 1980).

CHAPTER 10

1. Albert Camus, "Create Dangerously," in *Literature and the Arts: The Moral Issues,* H. Girvertz and R. Ross, eds. (Belmont, CA: Wadsworth, 1971), p. 51.
2. My last visit to Estrada Courts occurred in 1974. Since paintings fade and the themes go out of date, it is possible that the walls have not been spared by graffitists. A mural cannot protect a wall against graffiti indefinitely, but it can protect it for a time.
3. Edward Bruce and Forbes Watson, *Art in Federal Buildings, Volume 1: Mural Designs 1934–1936* (Washington, DC, Art in Federal Buildings, Inc., 1936), p. ix.
4. Grace Glueck, "Art in Public Places Stirs Widening Debate," *New York Times* (May 23, 1982), p. D1.
5. Community art by its very nature tends to be public art. However, public art does not qualify as community art unless there is direct input by the potential audience in its selection or creation.
6. James Marston Fitch, "The Forms of Plenty," *Columbia University Forum* (Summer 1963), pp. 4–8.
7. Moshe Safdie, *Beyond Habitat* (Montreal: Tundra Books, 1970), p. 167.
8. Ibid, p. 169.
9. Alma M. Reed, *The Mexican Muralists* (New York: Crown Publishers, 1960).
10. The insensitivity of most fine arts painting and sculpture to its surroundings has not always been the case, as Rudolf Arnheim explains in his book, *The Dynamics of Architectural Form.* Prior to the Renaissance, a painting used to be made for a particular wall of a particular building, and the meaning and function of a statue was controlled by its context.
11. Bruce and Watson, *Art in Federal Buildings,* p. 3.
12. Their efforts have produced film documentaries depicting the development of murals from start to completion, slide packets, mural maps, and tour guides showing the location of major wall paintings and information about date, title, artist, and materials. Slides and other materials can be purchased from Environmental Communications, 62 Windward Avenue, Venice, CA, 90291 and Ars Nova Media, Schlagergasse 5, A-1090, Wien, Austria. *Community Murals* (P. O. Box 40383, San Francisco, CA, 94140) is a periodical devoted specifically to community art.

CHAPTER 11

1. Ralph Nader, *Unsafe at Any Speed* (New York: Pocketbooks, 1966).
2. Stuart Chase and F. J. Schlink, *Your Money's Worth* (New York: MacMillan 1927).
3. Robert O. Herrmann, "The Consumer Movement in Historical Perspec-

tive," in *Consumerism,* 2nd ed., David A. Aaker and George S. Day, eds. (New York: Free Press), p. 12.

4. Aaker and Day, *Consumerism,* p. xvii.
5. Christian Norberg-Schultz, "Less or More?," *Architectural Review* (April 1968, CXL 111), pp. 257–258.
6. Barker, *Psychological Ecology.*
7. Information on these programs is available in *Resources in Environment and Behavior* (Willo P. White, ed.) published in 1979. This volume can be ordered from the American Psychological Association, 1200 17th St., NW, Washington, DC 20036.
8. Robert Sommer, *Personal Space* (Englewood Cliffs, NJ: Prentice-Hall, 1969).
9. Mitzi Ayala "The California Cornucopia," *Davis Daily Democrat,* February 25, 1981, p. B 3.
10. *Environment, 19*(6) (1977), p. 2.
11. Harland Manchester, "Mini-People, Inc.?," *Saturday Review* (October 1971), p. 6.
12. Thomas Whiteside, "Tomatoes," *New Yorker* (January 24, 1977), pp. 35–62.
13. Eleanor Randolph, "'Tomato War' Puts U.S. Negotiators in Squeeze," *Los Angeles Times,* September 10, 1979, p. 1.
14. Tad Thompson, "Reaction Mixed on Tomato Issue," *The Packer* (February 20, 1982), p. 3 A.
15. There is also scientific evidence that tomatoes purchased from small farmers taste better than supermarket tomatoes even when customers do not know the origin of the produce. In "double-blind" laboratory comparison, in which neither the experimenter nor the taster knew the origin of the fruit, farmers' market tomatoes were significantly preferred over supermarket tomatoes (Robert Sommer, Margot Stumpf, and Henry Bennett, "Quality of Farmers' Market Produce: Flavor and Pesticide Residues," *Jour. of Consumer Affairs, 16,* (1982), pp. 130–36.
16. Ron Butler, "In Search of the Perfect Tomato," *Western World* (March/April 1978), p. 31.
17. Whiteside, Tomatoes, p. 61.
18. Steve Duscha, "Our Strawberries Get Razzberries," *Sacramento Bee,* May 7, 1977, p. A 1.
19. Whiteside, Tomatoes.
20. Mario Dianda, "New Machine for Market Tomatoes," *Davis Daily Democrat,* July 30, 1977, p. 1.
21. Robert Sommer, *Farmers Markets of America* (Santa Barbara, CA: Capra 1980).

INDEX